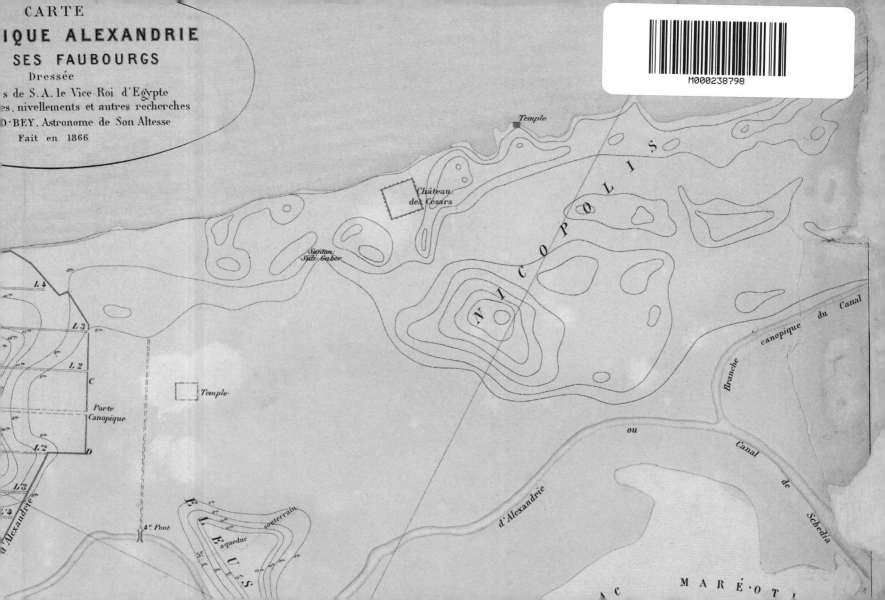

CARTE

...QUE ALEXANDRIE

ET SES FAUBOURGS

Dressée

...s de S. A. le Vice-Roi d'Egypte

...es, nivellements et autres recherches

...D-BEY, Astronome de Son Altesse

Fait en 1866

Temple

N I C O P O L I S

Château des Césars

Santon Sidi-Gaber

L 4

L 3

L 2

C

Porte Canopique

Temple

L'2

D

L'3

F I L E U S

4.e Pont

Aqueduc   souterrain

Branche   canopique du Canal

ou

Canal   de   Schedia

d'Alexandrie

L A C   M A R É O T I...

ALEXANDREA AD ÆGYPTUM

Endpapers: (Front) Map of Ancient Alexandria and its Suburbs drawn at the orders of H. H. the Viceroy of Egypt with the aid of excavations, levelling and other research by Mahmoud Bey, Astronomer to His Highness, in 1866. (Back) Alexandria, Map of the City, Ancient and Modern, Prof. M. Bartocci, circa 1914.

Published by Zeitouna
30 Abdine Square, Cairo, Egypt 11111

Dar el-Kutub nº 15273/2020
ISBN 978 977 5864 31 4

Printed in Egypt

ALEXANDREA AD ÆGYPTUM

edited by Sherif Boraïe

ZEITOUNA

THE CITY

You said: "I'll go to another country, go to another shore,
find another city better than this one.
Whatever I try to do is fated to turn out wrong
and my heart lies buried as though it were something dead.
How long can I let my mind moulder in this place?
Wherever I turn, wherever I happen to look,
I see the black ruins of my life, here,
where I've spent so many years, wasted them, destroyed
them totally."

You won't find a new country, won't find another shore.
This city will always pursue you. You will walk
the same streets, grow old in the same neighbourhoods, will turn gray in these same houses.
You will always end up in this city. Don't hope for things
elsewhere:
there is no ship for you, there is no road.
As you've wasted your life here, in this small corner,
you've destroyed it everywhere else in the world.

C. P. Cavafy

Eastern Harbour, Anna Boghiguian, ink on paper, 1998.

Statue of Mohamed Ali Pasha in Place des Consuls (Mohamed Ali Square), circa 1867.

Foreword

When Mohamed Ali became the Pasha of Egypt, the city of Alexander was a decrepit backwater with less than five thousand people.

Alexandria, the first cosmopolitan metropolis, centre of learning, repository of knowledge and emporium to the world had long been buried in ruins.

Like Alexander, Mohamed Ali was from Macedonia, born in the city of Kavala in northern Greece, then part of the Ottoman Empire, in a family of Albanian origin.

He arrived in Egypt in 1801 as second-in-command of an Albanian contingent, part of an Ottoman force sent to re-occupy the country after Napoleon Bonaparte's invasion in 1798.

By 1805, the wily soldier of fortune had become ruler of Egypt, anointed by the people and confirmed by the Ottoman Sultan.

In a short time, he built a new modern cosmopolitan Alexandria that became his unofficial capital.

The keys to his success were, first, the port which he resuscitated from oblivion, making it the hub of Egypt's trade and gateway to the world, to the detriment of Rosetta and Damietta.

He dug the Mahmoudieh Canal, connecting Alexandria to the Nile, bringing fresh water and produce from the Nile Delta and Valley, and cultivating the area around Alexandria.

He introduced cotton, which rapidly became Egypt's cash crop and Alexandria's path to prosperity.

He set up the *Commissione di Ornato*—like in Milan and Venice, and administered by Europeans—to plan the city and supervise the construction of roads and buildings.

And he imported and encouraged talent, rewarding it handsomely. French engineers and doctors, Italian architects and masons, Greek merchants and craftsmen, Syrian traders—from across the Mediterranean, the Ottoman Empire and further afield in Europe, people flocked to Alexandria where fortunes were made and all religions and races respected.

The new Alexandria was almost Greek with Italian colours and an Oriental touch. French was the lingua franca. The Egyptian elite, predominantly Turco-Circassian, happily indulged. An Egyptian migrant workforce served. Levantines pretended to be European. Maghrebians were sufi saints and traders. Jews could be found in all social strata.

Alexandrea ad Ægyptum, the old Latin adage meaning "next to" or "by" Egypt, re-emerged, underlining Alexandria's singular separateness. In effect, a colonial project formalised by British occupation in 1882.

The fatal blow to Alexandria was delivered by Gamal Abdel Nasser, the Egyptian army colonel who overthrew Farouk, the last king of Mohamed Ali's dynasty.

On 26 July, 1956, from the city's holy of holies, the parapet of the Bourse on Mohamed Ali Square, Nasser announced the nationalisation of the Suez Canal.

As the sizeable foreign community left, following the Suez War, then through waves of nationalisation, the international city was no more.

Alexandria, Georg Braun, 1645.

ALEXANDRIA.

MEDITERR   ANEVM   MARE

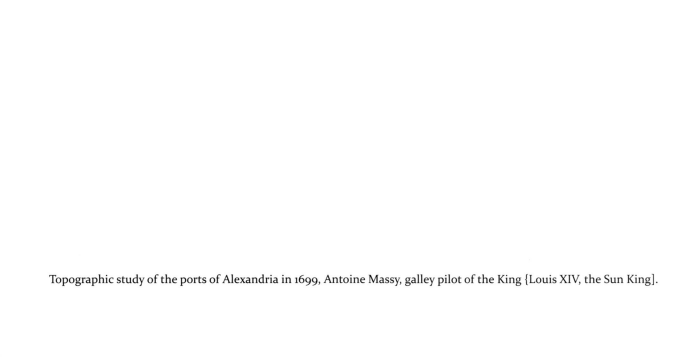

Topographic study of the ports of Alexandria in 1699, Antoine Massy, galley pilot of the King {Louis XIV, the Sun King].

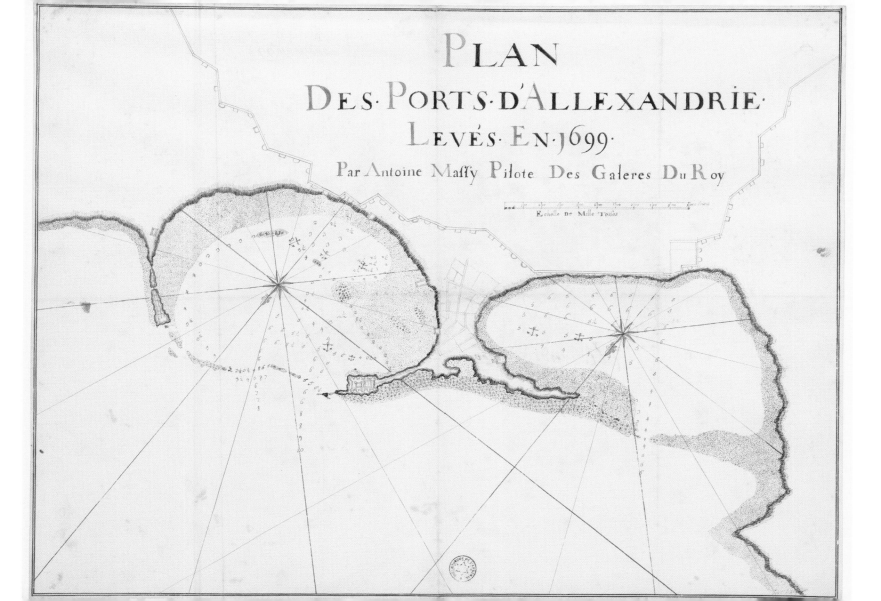

PLAN
DES·PORTS·D'ALLEXANDRIE·
LEVÉS·EN·1699·
Par Antoine Massy Pilote Des Galeres Du Roy

Echelle De Mille Toises

Plan of the Alexandria fort, called the Great Pharos, that defends the port's entrance, Étienne Gravier, 1685-1687.

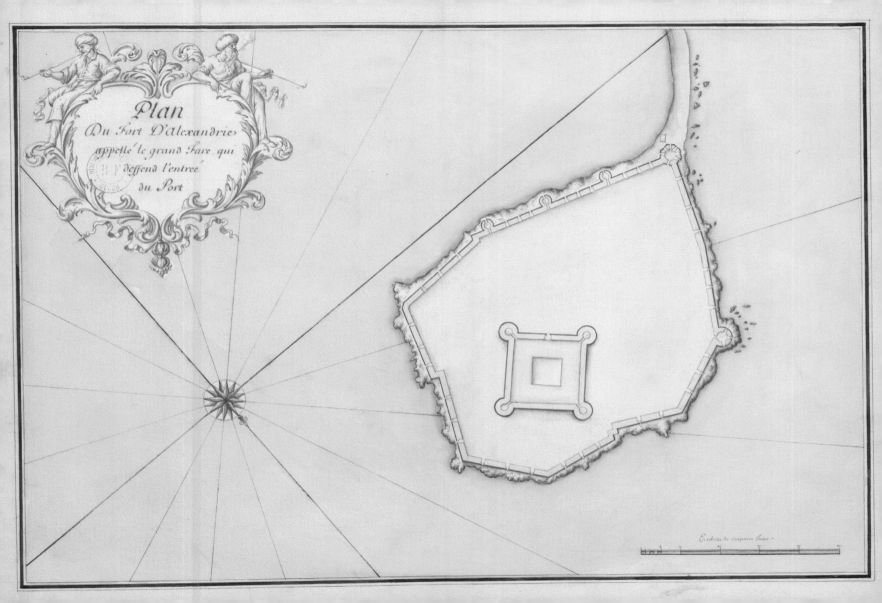

Plan

Du Fort D'Alexandrie
appellé le grand Fare, qui
deffend l'entrée
du Port

Eschelle de Cinquante toises

Plan of Alexandria, Jean-Baptiste Bourguignon d'Anville, 1697-1782.

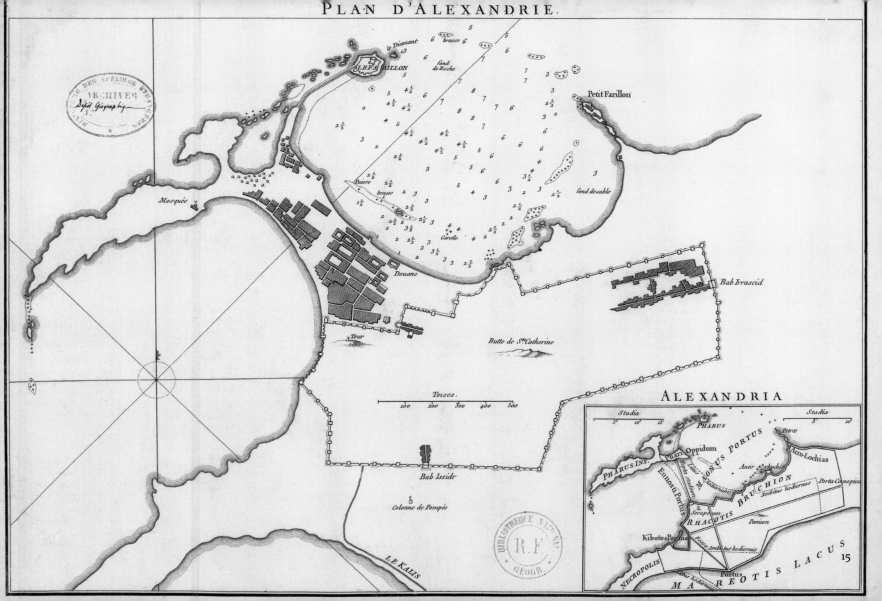

PLAN D'ALEXANDRIE.

le Diamant

ILE FARILLON

Petit Farillon

brasso

fond de Roche

Poivre

brasso

Gerolle

fond de sable

Mosquée

Douane

Bab Irrascid

Tour

Butte de St. Catherine

Toises.

100   200   300   400   500

Bab Issidr

Colonne de Pompée

LE KALIS

ALEXANDRIA

Stadia   Stadia

PHARUS

Oppidum

PHARUS INS.

Pharos

MAGNUS PORTUS

Petrœ

Acro-Lochias

Eunosti Portus

Serapeum

Heptastadium

Antir rhodus

BRUCHION

Ambitus hodiernus

Porta Canopica

RHACOTIS

Panium

Kibotos Portus

Fossa Ambitus hodiernus

NECROPOLIS

Portus

MA REOTIS LACUS

15

A plan of Alexandria dedicated to The Right Honourable William, Earl of Harrington, Lord President of the Council.

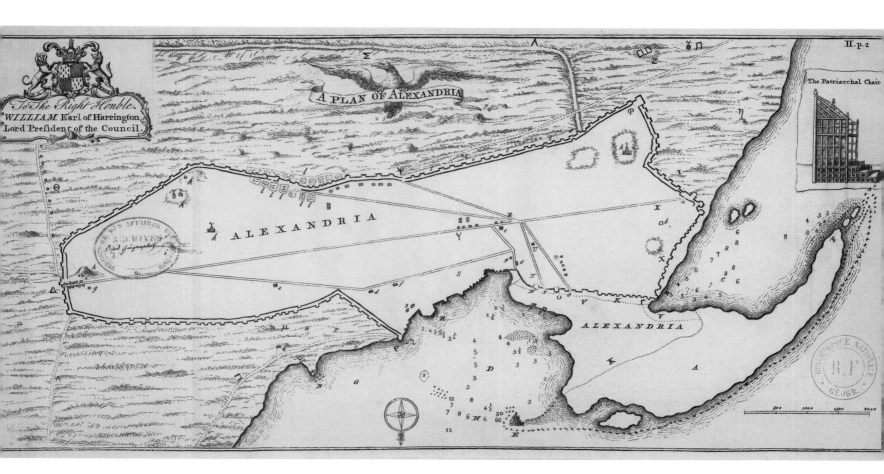

A PLAN OF ALEXANDRIA

To The Right Honble.
WILLIAM Earl of Harrington,
Lord Prefident of the Council.

The Patriarchal Chair

ALEXANDRIA

ALEXANDRIA

500   1000   1500   2000

Plan of the ports and city of Alexandria, Jacques-Nicolas Bellin, 1740-1745.

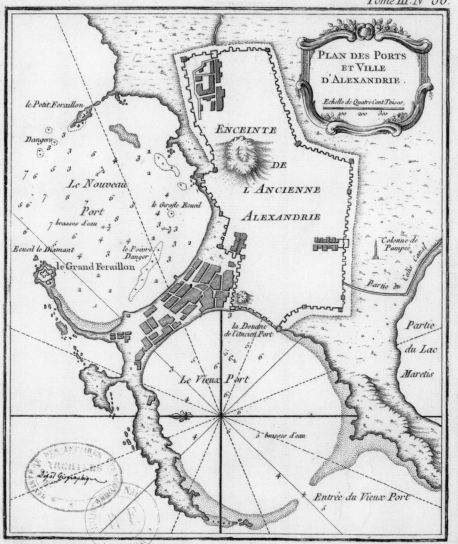

PLAN DES PORTS
ET VILLE
D'ALEXANDRIE.

Echelle de Quatre Cent Toises.
100   200   300

le Petit Feraillon

Dangers

Le Nouveau
Port

7 brasses d'eau

le Grosse Ecueil

Ecueil le Diamant
le Grand Feraillon

le Poivre
Danger

ENCEINTE
DE
L'ANCIENNE
ALEXANDRIE

Colonne de
Pompée

Partie du
Petit Canal

la Douane
de l'ancien Port

Le Vieux Port

Partie
du Lac
Maretis

Entrée du Vieux Port

3 brasses d'eau

19

Patriarchatus Alexandrinus, A. Robert, Paris, 1743.

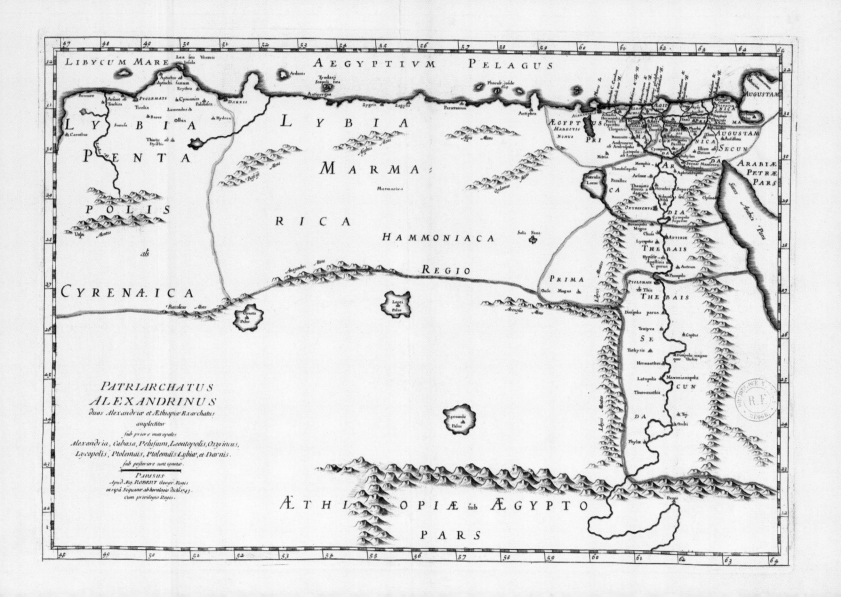

PATRIARCHATUS ALEXANDRINUS

Coast of Egypt from Alexandria to Rosetta, Jacques-Nicolas Bellin, 1740-1749.

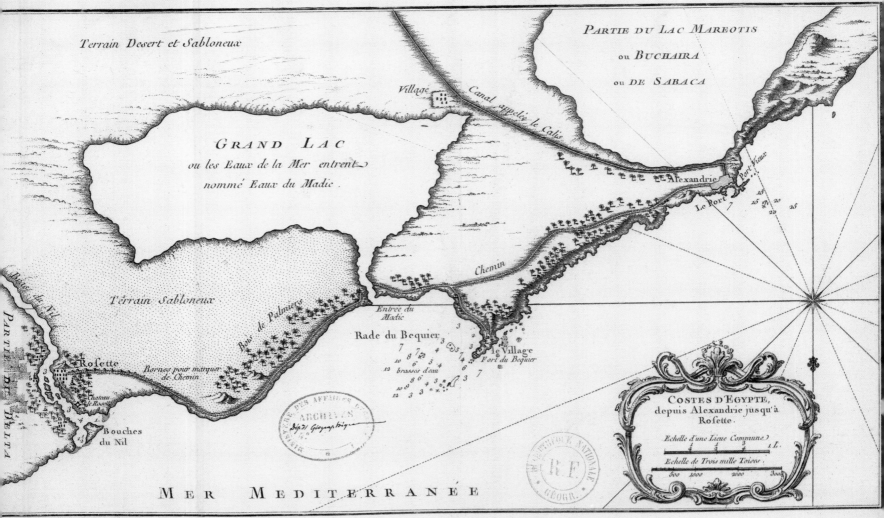

Terrain Desert et Sabloneux

PARTIE DU LAC MAREOTIS

ou BUCHAIRA

ou DE SABACA

Village *Canal appelé le Calis*

GRAND LAC

ou les Eaux de la Mer entrent
nommé Eaux du Madic.

Alexandrie *Port Vieux*

Le Port

15
15 20 25
20

Chemin

Terrain Sabloneux

Bras du Nil

Bois de Palmiers

Entrée du Madic

Rade du Bequier 3

PARTIE DU DELTA

7 3
7 4 5 3
10 8 6 5 3
12 brasses d'eau 3
7

Le Village
Fort du Bequier

Rosette

Bornes pour marquer de Chemin

10 8 6 3
12

Chateau de Rosette

Bouches du Nil

MER MEDITERRANÉE

COSTES D'EGYPTE,
depuis Alexandrie jusqu'à
Rosette.

Echelle d'une Lieue Commune.
4 4 1 L.

Echelle de Trois mille Toises.
500 1000 2000 3000

Map of the city of Alexandria and of Minet-el-Bassal, by C. Marchettini, 1890,
approved and adopted by Insurance Companies in their general assembly of 16 March 1885.

Plan de la Ville d'ALEXANDRIE et du Marché de Minet-el-Bassal nouvellement dressé par Ing.-Chev. C. Marchettini 1890

Approuvé et Adopté par les Compagnies d'assurances dans leur assemblée générale du 16 Mars 1885

Echelle de 1/6000

ANNÉE 1891

GRAND PORT EST

GRAND PORT DE MOUILLAGE

ANCIEN PORT DES ROMAINS

Les Chiffres près des quais indiquent le mouillage des Bateaux

Canal Mahmoudieh

LÉGENDE DES COULEURS

Bâtisses publiques
Bâtisses privées
Bâtisses en fer
Terrains soumis aux fortifications
Eaux
Jardins
Chemin de fer

General Plan of Alexandria and its recent establishments, Alexandre Nicohosoff, 1930.

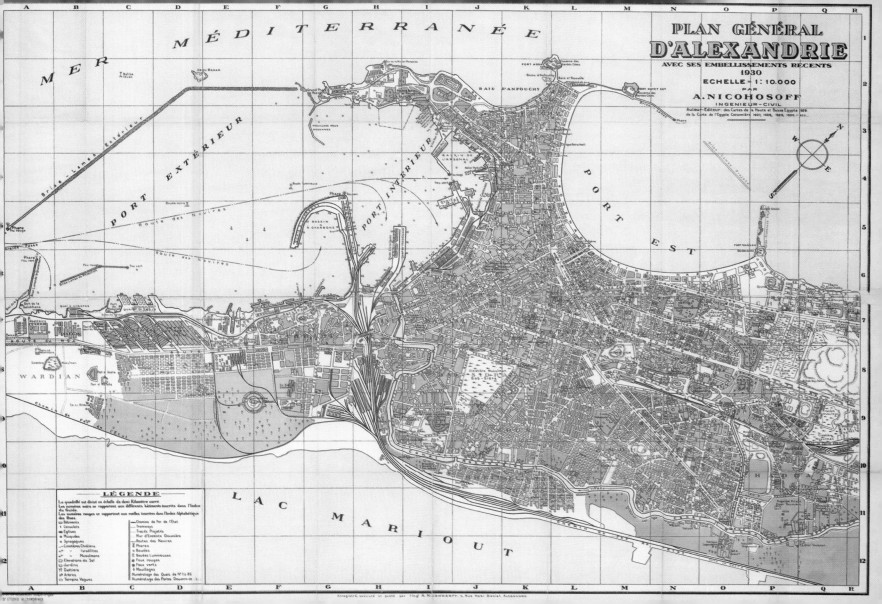

PLAN GÉNÉRAL D'ALEXANDRIE
AVEC SES EMBELLISSEMENTS RÉCENTS
1930
ECHELLE = 1 : 10.000
PAR
A. NICOHOSOFF
INGENIEUR–CIVIL

Auteur-Editeur: des Cartes de la Haute et Basse Egypte 1929.
de la Carte de l'Egypte Cotonnière 1927, 1928, 1929, 1930... etc...

MER MÉDITERRANÉE

BAIE D'ANFOUCHY

PORT EXTÉRIEUR

PORT INTÉRIEUR

PORT EST

WARDIAN

LAC MARIOUT

LÉGENDE

La quadrillé est divisé en échelle de demi Kilomètre carré.
Les numéros noirs se rapportent aux différents bâtiments inscrits dans l'Index du Guide.
Les numéros rouges se rapportent aux ruelles inscrites dans l'Index Alphabétique des Rues.

Bâtiments
Consulats
Eglises
Mosquées
Synagogues
Cimetières Chrétiens
"   "   Israélites
Elevations du Sol
Jardins
Dattiers
Arbres
Terrains Vagues

Chemins de Fer de l'Etat
Tramways
Tracés Projetés
Mur d'Enceinte Douanière
Routes des Navires
Phares
Bouées
Bouées Lumineuses
Feux rouges
Feux verts
Mouillages
Numérotage des Quais de N° 1 à 88
Numérotage des Portes Douanes de 1 à

The British Bombardment of Alexandria

July 11, 1882.

The Prime Minister Mr. Gladstone had a personal incentive for intervening, as he realised when adding up his fortune in December 1881. He had an exceptionally large holding in Egyptian government bonds: £40,567 or 37% of his entire portfolio. Sixty-five other MP's also had investments in Egypt. Thanks in part to the British occupation of Egypt, these investments would prove more profitable than many British stocks. The need to 'protect the Suez canal' was another factor influencing British policy. Strategy, 'the market' and domestic politics drove Britain to occupy Egypt. The fate of the Khedive, and of Europeans in Alexandria, would be a pretext.

On 20 May 1882 British and French gun boats anchored off Alexandria. Their orders were to communicate with the consuls- general, support the Khedive and land a force if the safety of Europeans required it. For the Khedive Europe was a friend - for most Egyptians an enemy. Many wanted a written constitution to replace khedivial absolutism.

On 13 June, as he did every year, the Khedive Tewfik arrived in Alexandria for the summer, accompanied by the foreign consuls-general and Egyptian ministers including the Minister of War, a popular hero called Urabi Pasha. Fighting between Egyptians and Europeans broke out. Most Europeans fled. On 11 July British warships opened fire on the city. That day and the next the main sounds in Alexandria were the crackle and roar of flames, the crash of falling buildings, and howling dogs. The last Egyptian troops left around 1 pm on 12 July.

Alexandria turned, in the words of a British consular assistant A. Hulme Beaman, into 'a dantesque Inferno, alight almost from end to end, the flames running riot from street to street without any attempt being made to check them being made, with wild figures here and there pillaging and looting and ghastly corpses swollen to gigantic proportions lying charred and naked in the roadways.' The only object untouched was the statue of Mohammed Ali, who seemed to survey the ruins with disgust.

Philip Mansel, *The Rise and Fall of Royal Alexandria: From Mohammed Ali to Farouk*, 2012.

The Palace of Count Zizinia, Place des Consuls (Mohamed Ali Square).

Place des Consuls (Mohamed Ali Square), right side.

Rue Cherif Pasha.

Rue Sesostris.

Rue Mosquée Attarine.

The Port of Alexandria

Dr. Sandro Breccia

1926

Geographical Position

The port of Alexandria occupies an exceptional situation at the end of a very large bay, measuring 10 kilometres in length and two kilometres in width, at the western tip of the Nile Delta. The depths of the waters near to the coastline are extremely favourable. In fact, depths of 55 metres are to be found as far distant as three miles. The coordinates of the Lighthouse positioned on Ras el-Tin point are latitude 31°11′43″ North and longitude 29°51′40″ East relative to the Greenwich meridian. Anchorage outside the port is possible at depths of 16 metres.

The average depth inside the port is 11 metres. The bay is not subject to any substantial silting up. Deposits introduced by the Mahmoudieh Canal are insignificant. A double track railway from the port provides the connection with Cairo or more accurately with the whole of Egypt. The Mahmoudieh Canal joins the port to the Nile, but has become completely inadequate as a means of transportation.

History

From a historical point of view we cannot speak of one "port" but of the several "harbours" of Alexandria. Although literary tradition tells us of a "well-sheltered harbour" existing on the island of Pharos at the time of Homer, in reality the city founded by the Macedonian conqueror has, since its foundation, always possessed more than one harbour. Moreover, although commercial activity today is concentrated in the West Port or Old Port, the East Port still exists and it is intended to use it on a larger scale than at present.

Until the end of the fourth century BC, the coastline on which Alexander the Great founded the new capital of Egypt differed considerably from the one we now recognise. A large sea inlet, approximately 1,200 metres wide at its narrowest point, separated the mainland from the isle of Pharos. This islet, no more than 1,300,000 square metres in area, would have played an important role at an even earlier time than this, namely 1200 BC and even before. As I have previously mentioned, Homer, in the Odyssey, alludes to the harbour on this island, where the sailors came to replenish their drinking water. About fifteen years ago Mr. Jondet, former Chief Engineer of Ports and Lighthouses, discovered in the North West and in the South of the island "submerged remains of elaborate maritime engineering, incontrovertible proof of the existence of ancient harbours."

In truth, some archaeologists have disputed their existence. Mr. Dussaud believes this is quite simply erosion due to the action of the waves over millennia. Mr. Dussaud did not have the opportunity to verify in situ the information given by the Chief Engineer, Mr. Jondet, and he is wrong to deny the existence of man-made works; nonetheless, there are good reasons to seriously doubt the very great antiquity that has been assigned them.

Mr. Jondet thought that the construction of these contested harbours could be traced back to King Ramses II, renowned monument builder. Weill, Evans, Glotz and others preferred to believe that the creators of the harbour at Pharos were not Egyptian but Cretans of the Minoan era. All of these assertions are purely hypothetical and highly debatable. It may well be that these quays, 15 metres in width, spread over a total of 4 kilometres, are not from genuine harbours, but were simply breakwaters, the first "defensive quays" referred to by the historian Joseph Flavius, constructed in the Graeco-Roman era to protect the island of Pharos from the breaking waves and to provide a well-sheltered refuge for ships anchored in the harbours of Alexandria. It ill behoves us to simply

Port of Alexandria: The quays, circa 1890.

dismiss Mr. Jondet's discovery, since it had lasting repercussions throughout the scientific world and among the general public, exaggerating its importance, not only its relatively high archaeological importance, but also its much lower historical importance.

In reality, the history of the harbour at Alexandria begins at the end of the fourth century. The new plan of the city, designed by the architect Dinocrates, presaged the creation of two vast and magnificent harbour basins. In order to achieve this, a mighty causeway, measuring 1,200 metres in length from the southern point of the island of Pharos to the mainland, was required: the renowned Heptastadium.

Of the two harbour basins thus formed, that of the East or Great Harbour became the principal harbour, and that of the South-West, Eunostos, was of secondary importance during the Graeco-Roman era. Contained within Eunostos, there was also another much less conspicuous harbour known as 'Strongbox', possibly serving a military purpose. A navigable canal crossed the city area, one branch of which flowed into the East Harbour and another branch into Eunostos Harbour, not far from the mouth of the existing Mahmoudieh Canal. One final port existed inland, on Lake Mareotis. This inland port was the centre of trade between Alexandria and part of Lower Egypt, and principally between the then very prosperous Mareotic region, the Siwa Oasis and Libya.

It is widely known that, because of its wonderful location almost at the centre of the then-civilized world, on the edge of the Mediterranean, its good connections not only with the rich Nile Valley, but also with regions in the Red Sea and India, Alexandria soon became a universal emporium, a marketplace for the entire world. During the Roman occupation, its importance remained high and even increased.

The main products exported were wheat, slaves, salted meats, birds, rare animals, wild beasts, glass, crystal, woven linen fabric, carpets, jewellery, coloured marble, papyrus, and books written on papyrus.

The decline began towards the third century AD, for a wide range of reasons, including disputes between the Alexandrians. The Byzantine Empire was in perpetual religious turmoil, and the focus of the most appalling disorder was the great, tumultuous and cosmopolitan city of Alexandria. However, we know that in the sixth century the port of Alexandria remained one of the principal trading stations of the world.

In 641 Alexandria was conquered by the Arabs, who transferred the capital of the country first to Fustat and later to Misr el-Qahira (Cairo). The former Queen of the Mediterranean obviously did not profit by this either in terms of prosperity or in importance. Nevertheless the port endured as an extremely important centre of trade throughout the Middle Ages. The Venetians, Amalfitans, and Genoese were first to establish regular shipping routes and enjoy trading privileges with Alexandria.

There is an account of up to twenty-eight nations having trade relations with Alexandria in the Middle Ages. There was still considerable prosperity up to 1483, but a definitive decline occurred soon thereafter. Among the main causes were:

1. The discovery of America (1492), the new and very rich continent, which stimulated Europe's interest and avarice.
2. The conquest of Egypt by the Ottoman Turks, whose maladministration impoverished the country.
3. The expansion of trade in goods by the Portuguese, who, having discovered the route to India by the Cape of Good Hope, competed successfully with Alexandria, the previous holder of that monopoly.

The abandonment of the port was so complete that in the seventeenth and eighteenth centuries the metropolis, whose population had reached 1 million, was reduced to a village of five or six thousand inhabitants languishing on the narrow strip of land formed over

Alexandrie. — Comptoir Philatélique d'Egypte

305   EGYPTE. — La Douane d'Alexandrie

جمرُك اسكَنْدرِيّة

Port of Alexandria: The Customs.

centuries on the site of the ancient Heptastadium (Rue Franque and Rue Ras el-Tin).

The nineteenth century saw the miracle of its rebirth which represents one of the triumphs of the great Mohamed Ali.

On 9 July, French Admiral Brueys wrote to the *Directoire* in these terms: "It is vexing that there is no harbour in Alexandria where a squadron may enter; but the much vaunted ancient port is enclosed by reefs above the water which form very narrow channels between which there is only twenty-three, twenty-five and fifty feet of water."

Less than a quarter of a century after this date, Mohamed Ali arranged for the repair and cleaning of the canal supplying fresh water to Alexandria and providing a waterway connection with the interior. Without this canal and access to its safe drinking water, the city of Alexandria could not have existed. The ancient port possessed only two wooden pontoons. At Ras el-Tin point, Mohamed Ali first commissioned an arsenal and then a lighthouse, and near to the lighthouse he built a palace residence.

Works on the arsenal were planned and controlled by engineer Mr. Lefèvre de Cerisy. Mr. Mougel, the successor to Mr. Cerisy, managed the construction of the first dry dock. From 1819 to 1849 (the death of Mohamed Ali), commercial activity at the port increased enormously and its population reached 100,000 inhabitants.

In 1854, under Saïd Pasha, construction of the railway joining Alexandria to Cairo was started and under Ismail Pasha, progress was enormous. By 1866 the population had risen to 250,000 inhabitants. In 1869 a Commission chaired by Linant de Bellefonds approved the following works:
1. Large breakwaters 2,340 metres in length, starting from Ras el-Tin.
2. A mole or dyke 1,020 metres in length, starting at Gabbari.
3. A dry dock for cargo ships.

4. New very-deep-water quays.

The execution of these works was entrusted to William Bruce Greenfield and Company, who by 1880 had completed them. Total expenditure amounted to 75,284,000 French francs. Between 1880 and 1890 the length of the coal wharf grew from 30 to 90 metres, quays lengthened, Customs stores multiplied, the railway line branched out.

Two navigational buoys, built at Mex in 1890 but only operational from 1894, were made for the Boghaz Channel. This channel was excavated to a depth of 30 feet, straightened and extended to 300 feet.

The major works executed between 1900 and 1917 completely transformed the appearance of the older harbour and the bay.

The external breakwater was extended by 600 metres. The new quarantine pier, 415 metres long, was built. The protective breakwater for the coal wharf was further increased in size from 90 to 130 metres. Numerous railway lines crossed the quayside. Seven steam-powered cranes each loaded the coal hulks with 350 tonnes per day.

The dry dock at Gabbari, excavated out of the rock, measures 158 metres in length and is capable of accepting vessels with a draft of 7 metres. Timber stores, which were inside the harbour, were transferred to the dry dock and the quarantine pier at Gabbari and even further away at Souk el-Wardian.

All oil trading activities were also removed from within the city and transferred to Gabbari. In the inner harbour, old piers have been widened and equipped with storehouses, the Arsenal Basin was considerably improved and, most recently, an enormous completely new mole was constructed, setting vast areas of quayside upon the sea.

These works necessitated an expenditure of about 3 million Egyptian pounds. To have an idea of the extraordinary progress made over one century, we need simply consider that in 1915 the port of Alexandria

Port of Alexandria: Entrance to the Customs.

was able to offer safe haven to 137 vessels, both merchant and military, some weighing between 20,000 and 30,000 tonnes, but still able to navigate to the docks. This is without taking into account a further 77 sailing vessels consigned to the Ras el-Tin area and the great outer breakwater. And we are now in the fortunate position of announcing that Egypt's main port no longer meets its shipping needs. And we are right to expect congratulations for this, because Alexandria Harbour is endowed with all the attributes necessary to accommodate any increase in business at the port for the foreseeable future. To this end, convinced of the absolutely strict necessity of immediately easing the current congestion, and planning for the near future, the Egyptian government has planned new works. A committee of experts has been appointed to deliberate. Expenditure for these works, which are to start imminently, is expected to be 3 million Egyptian pounds.

Lighthouses

There has been an operational lighthouse at Ras el-Tin point since 1844. The cylindrical tower, 55 metres in height, has a prismatic lantern with 24 rotating faces and a revolving light powered by paraffin vapour, giving flashes at 20-second intervals, visible from 20 miles distant.

Other secondary lighthouses and navigational buoys shine along the coastline at Mex. The entrance to the harbour comprises two main channels: the Great Channel and the Boghaz Channel.

The direction of each of these two channels is indicated by the alignment of the two lighthouses located on the coast of Mex with a third, the Great Lighthouse of Mex, standing at the top of the angle formed by the two channels.

The harbour is protected by two converging breakwaters, 3,500 metres and 635 metres long respectively, which leaves an opening of 400 metres. The harbour is divided into two sections from south-east to north-west by the large coal wharf and the small inner breakwater; the western section is called the Outer Harbour; the eastern, closest to town, the Inner Harbour.

Topography and technical organization

The current area of water is 750 hectares, of which 510 return to the Outer Harbour and 240 to the Inner Harbour. To enter or leave the harbour, ships are obliged to use a pilot, whose responsibility starts from the point beyond the outer lighthouse situated on the large breakwater, up to the inner part of the coal wharf and, of course, vice-versa.

Around the Inner Harbour, going from east to west we find:
1. Administration of Ports and Lighthouses.
2. Quarantine Administration.
3. Customs Administration.
4. Tobacco warehouses.
5. Bonded stores, etc.

Between the aforementioned buildings and the sea protrudes a line of storage buildings provided for those shipping companies with regular services to Egypt. The entire port is provided with quayside areas measuring 78 hectares. The total length of the quays is 12,137 kilometres. The length of docks with 7- to 9-metre berths is 7,300 kilometres. The average width of the quays is 459 feet.

Eighty-two ships can both berth and unload at the docks. The harbour is comfortably able to accommodate 250 boats.

Technical management is entrusted to the Harbour Master's office. Commercial management to Customs Administration. Handling to the Ports and Lighthouses Administration.

The port is fitted with dry docks, a rescue tug with a capacity of 600 horsepower, and a pump boat with a pumping capacity 240 tonnes of water per hour.

Port of Alexandria.

The Quarantine office presides over the operation of four quarantine holding pens and an isolation house located between Gabbari and Mex.

All railway lines converge outside the confines of the port, at the goods station in Gabbari.

The total length of railway lines along the quays is 20 km.

The Mahmoudieh Canal, which separates from the so-called Rosetta branch of the Nile, has its head near Fouah and empties into the harbour after a journey of 80 kilometres.

The depth of the channel is no more than 2.70 metres and its width varies from 25 to 40 metres. As we have already said, navigation is slow and difficult. It is a matter of extreme urgency to improve the state of this canal, already of great importance to the port of Alexandria, and likely to become even more so.

Storage Hangars

These are State-owned storage buildings authorised for use by traders, which today are forty-four in number, with an area of 106,983 m².

The Bonded Store Co. Ltd. owns four large warehouses and two smaller ones with reinforced cement floors: an area totalling 20,000 m², not including those warehouses outside the Customs Area used for goods on which Customs duty has been paid.

The lighting of quays and on the quaysides is provided by 400 gas lamps. The Alexandria Water Company supplies drinking water for ships at a cost of 3 ¾ piastres per m3; for ships at a distance from the quays, the price is 12 piastres.

All vessels are subject to charges for:
1. Lighthouse
2. Tonnage
3. Wharfage
4. Pilotage

Customs Clearance

Provided that the Egyptian Government, in diplomatic discussions undertaken for the purpose, does not give prior consent to any modification by international agreement, Customs duty for import as well as export are fixed for the present time until 1930. This convention commits the Government of Egypt not to impose on farm and industrial products any taxes exceeding 8% ad valorem, except for fortified or aromatic alcohols (liqueurs) containing not more than 50 degrees of alcohol (10% ad valorem). Alcohols above 50 degrees, crude oil and animals can be taxed up to 15% ad valorem.

To avoid disputes and difficulties between Customs and traders, price tariffs for various goods have been set up in common agreement. These tariffs remain in force for a period of one year.

Regarding export, a duty of 1% ad valorem must be paid for all agricultural or industrial products from Egypt, in addition to an Export Quays Dues tax, which is paid at a rate of 12% on general goods.

The Egyptian Bonded Warehouses Co. Ltd. manages the General Stores (Bonded Stores or Docks). This company oversees all operations concerning the receiving of goods, customs clearance, and the handling and consigning of all merchandise, issuing for this purpose "Warehouse Certificates" and "Transfer Orders."

Scale of Shipping and Trade

With regard to the tonnage of goods, Alexandria ranks third among all Mediterranean ports, coming immediately after Marseilles and Genoa. The total value of shipping (both import and export) in the years following the Great War tends to stabilise between 80 and 100 million Egyptian pounds (L.E.). Exports far exceed imports. In 1924 the latter amounted to L.E. 41,163,549 while exports exceeded L.E. 64 million.

Port of Alexandria: Port and Customs.

The 1925 statistics give the following figures:
Imports L.E. 58,224,895; gold and silver L.E. 617,036.

Exports L.E. 59,198,662; gold and silver L.E. 93,140.

Trans-shipment L.E. 853,280.

Re-export L.E. 1,270,174.

Egyptian trade has until now been concentrated for the most part in the Port of Alexandria. In fact 95–99% of all exports and 80–82% of all imports are attributable to this port.

The few figures that I have just quoted indicate with striking eloquence the importance of the port of Alexandria for the economic life of Egypt. And it is not beyond the realms of possibility to imagine even greater trading activity in the near future.

Egypt, which today has a population of around 13 million inhabitants, can easily feed up to 20 million, a figure it will reach in less than 30 years. The fellahin, on the other hand, will not delay in wanting to improve their living conditions, and there is no doubting that an industrial Egypt will also grow and prosper quickly alongside an agricultural Egypt. We must also bear in mind that the dramatic growth of Egypt's neighbouring countries (Syria, Palestine, Arabia) will present an opportunity to increase the volume of trading through trans-shipments.

In summary then, there are many prospects for ever-increasing activity at this wonderful Port of Alexandria whose history guarantees an ever-increasing prosperity for the future.

Port of Alexandria: New Docks.

Ras el-Tin Lighthouse. "There has been an operational lighthouse at Ras el-Tin point since 1844. The cylindrical tower, 55 metres in height, has a prismatic lantern with 24 rotating faces and a revolving light powered by paraffin vapour, giving flashes at 20-second intervals, visible from 20 miles distant." —Sandro Breccia, *The Port of Alexandria*, 1926.

Ras el-Tin Lighthouse.

Ras el-Tin Palace

The summer palace of Ras el-Tin at Alexandria stands on the promontory of that name—part of the ancient island of Pharos, which has long since been welded to the mainland. The palace is a long, narrow block of buildings running east and west and divided by central corridors. Under its northern windows lie beautiful gardens, shaded by palm and acacia, glowing with flowers of rare scent and splendour, freshened with cool streams and fountains; and beyond the gardens one hears the gentle plash of waves, and looks over the purple waters of the Mediterranean. On the southern side the palace, walls are washed by the peaceful billows of the great harbour, which presents an ever-changing picture, as the great ships come and go, or tiny Arab boats scud across its glimmering surface. Altogether a more charming situation cannot be imagined; and the charm once felt can never be forgotten.

Alfred Joshua Butler, *Court Life in Egypt*, 1887.

ALEXANDRIE _ PALAIS DE RAS-EL-TIN.

Ras el-Tin Palace.

Mohamed Ali built a palace on the western edge of the peninsula on which Alexandria was built, called Ras el-Tin (the cape of figs) in 1811–17. It was in traditional Ottoman style, in wood and plaster, with wide, projecting eaves, and protruding rectangular windows, probably designed by craftsmen from the mountains of Macedonia. There were two sections: a harem, like a walled convent; and a divan or office and reception building. Soon, however, reflecting the influence of an architect from Livorno called Pietro Avoscani, the palace began to look more European. Portraits of Mohamed Ali's own family and European monarchs were hung on the walls, French furniture placed in the rooms.

In Ras el-Tin the pasha kept open house. Foreigners were more likely to be present in the palace than pious Muslims. A French consul wrote that Mohamed Ali had bought most of the ulama; those opposed to his projects were exiled. Once one of the most fanatical provinces of the Ottoman Empire, under Mohamed Ali Egypt became one of its most tolerant. Jabarti complained that Christians, 'the enemies of our religion', had become 'the companions and intimate friends of His Highness', and even employed Muslims as servants.

King Fouad commissioned the transformation of Ras el-Tin palace, and the creation of a throne room in 'Islamic Baroque', by the architect of the royal palaces, his friend Ernesto Verrucci Bey.

Philip Mansel, *The Rise and Fall of Royal Alexandria: From Mohamed Ali to Farouk*, 2012.

104 *ALEXANDRIA.* — *Ras-El-Tin Palace.* — *LL*

Ras el-Tin Palace.

Entrance to Ras el-Tin Palace.

ALEXANDRIA. — Entrance to Ras-El-Tin Palace. — LL.

Entrance to Ras el-Tin Palace.

Ras el-Tin Palace.

Alexandrie.   *Palais "Ras-el-Tin".*

Ras el-Tin Palace.

South portico of Ras el-Tin Palace.

A reception hall in Ras el-Tin Palace.

Salon in Ras el-Tin Palace.

Interior detail of a room in Ras el-Tin Palace.

Fort Kait Bey (The "Pharos")

This battered and neglected little peninsula is perhaps the most interesting spot in Alexandria, for here, rising to an incredible height, once stood the Pharos Lighthouse, the wonder of the world. Contrary to general belief, some fragments of the Pharos still remain.

(1). The original building.
The lighthouse took its name from Pharos Island (hence the French "phare" and the Italian "faro"). No doubt it entered into Alexander the Great's scheme for his maritime capital, but the work was not done till the reign of Ptolemy Philadelphus. Probable date of dedication: B.C. 279, when the king held a festival to commemorate his parents. Architect: Sostratus, an Asiatic Greek. The sensation it caused was tremendous. It appealed both to the sense of beauty and to the taste for science—an appeal typical of the age. Poets and engineers combined to praise it. Just as the Parthenon had been identified with Athens and St. Peter's was to be identified with Rome, so, to the imagination of contemporaries, the Pharos became Alexandria and Alexandria became the Pharos. Never, in the history of architecture, has a secular building been thus worshipped and taken on a spiritual life of its own. It beaconed to the imagination, not only to ships at sea, and long after its light was extinguished memories of it glowed in the minds of men.

(2) History of the Building.
We must now follow this masterpiece of engineering into ages of myth and oblivion. It retained its form and functions unimpaired up to the Arab Conquest (A.D. 641). The first, and irreparable, disaster was the fall of the lantern (about 700), entailing the loss of scientific apparatus that could not be replaced. There is a legend that the disaster was planned by the Byzantine Emperor, who could not attack Egypt owing to the magic "Mirror," which detected or destroyed his ships. He sent an agent who gained the Caliph's confidence and told him that beneath the Pharos the treasure of Alexander the Great lay buried. The Caliph commenced demolition, and before the inhabitants of Alexandria, who knew better, could intervene, the two upper stories had fallen into the sea. Henceforth the Pharos is only a stump with a bonfire on the top.

(3). Fort Kait Bey.
For a hundred years ruins cumbered the peninsula. Then (1480) the Mameluke Sultan Kait Bey fortified it as part of his coast defence against the Turks, who had taken Constantinople and were threatening Egypt. Kait Bey is a great figure at Cairo, where mosques commemorate his glorious reign. Here he only builds a fort, but like all his work it is architecturally fine, and even in decay its outlines are harmonious. The scheme was a pentagon and in the enclosed area, on the exact site of the Pharos, stood a square castle or keep with a mosque embedded in it. The Turks effected their conquest in 1517, and when their power in its turn declined, Mohamed Ali (1805–1848) modernised the defences. No visitors were admitted, and the Fort gained the reputation of an impregnable and mysterious place. Its career ended with the English bombardment of 1882.

E. M. Forster, *Alexandria: A History and a Guide*, 1922.

Fort Kait Bey.

Aboul Abbas el-Mursi

The patron saint of Alexandria was born in A.D. 1219 in the town of Murcia, Valencia in Andalusia, which was then ruled by the Almoravid dynasty.

The son of a merchant, at the age of 24, he travelled with his family on a pilgrimage to Mecca. A shipwreck off the coast of North Africa claimed the lives of his parents. He and his elder brother settled in Tunis where he soon met Aboul Hassan el-Shazli, the famed Muslim mystic and founder of the preeminent Shazlia Sufi sect, and became his disciple.

Aboul Abbas travelled with Aboul Hassan to Egypt where they settled, spreading their spiritual teaching. Before his death, Aboul Hassan confirmed Aboul Abbas as his heir. Aboul Abbas taught for some 40 years until his death.

He was first buried in the Bab el-Bahr Cemetery until the chief merchant of Alexandria built him a domed mausoleum; a mosque and a minaret soon followed. Additions and reconstructions continued until King Fouad in 1929 instructed the government to build a new mosque and not to spare expenses. Its 9-metre 16-ton granite columns were imported from Italy. The new mosque, designed by Eugenio Valzania and developed by Mario Rossi, was built between 1928 and 1938.

from Radames Lackany, *Quatre Espagnols à Alexandrie au Moyen Age.*

The Mosque of Aboul Abbas el-Mursi.

The Eastern Harbour.

The Post and the Eastern Harbour.

The Modern Town

Evaristo Breccia
1922

E non il flutto del deserto urtante
e non la fuga dei barbarici anni
valse a domare quella balda figlia
del greco eroe.
Alacre industre a la sua terza vita
ella sorgea, sollecitando i fati.
CARDUCCI, *Odi Barbare, Alessandria*

Population. According to the last census (1917), the population of Alexandria amounts to approximately 435,000 inhabitants. As for the elements and nationalities that compose it, it is true to say, *mutatis mutandis*, that the conditions of the Graeco-Roman epoch are closely parallelled; once more Alexandria can be defined as a cosmopolitan city. Nearly 70,000 foreigners can be counted amongst her inhabitants, of whom about 30,000 are Greeks, more than 20,000 Italians, and several thousand French, English and other British subjects (Maltese, Indians), Austrians, Germans, Syrians, and Armenians; there are also certain numbers of Turks, Swiss, Spaniards, Americans, natives of Barbary and of Morocco, and Russians. Each country is represented by a Consul.

From a religious point of view, variety is no less marked. The majority is naturally Mussulman, but there are also many Catholics of different rites, many members of the Orthodox Church, Protestants, Israelites, etc. All the religions represented in Egypt have churches or temples at Alexandria: for some indeed Alexandria is the principal seat of religious authority.

One might be inclined to believe that such a variety of races, languages, religions, and manners could not constitute a town whose essential qualities are precisely tolerance and reciprocal respect. Alexandria, however, is a proof that much prejudice and racial hatred, much chauvinism, much religious fanaticism may grow milder, and may even disappear, when a race or a nationality has occasion to live in daily contact with other races and other nationalities, and can learn that each one of them has qualities that cannot but be appreciated and faults that may be tolerated.

Should any misfortune take place in one section of the population it is considered as a misfortune to the others too, and all with touching unanimity try their utmost to remedy it. Each retains his political, social and moral ideal, but they all respect that of others, and no one insists that his is the best or the finest and that it ought to govern the world.

Such, briefly, is the admirable state of things in Alexandria with regard to the social relations of the inhabitants. It is evident that among so many sections there are sure to be elements that leave much to be desired, but let us hasten to add, to the credit of the town, that in proportion to the number of its inhabitants, crimes committed in Alexandria are inferior in number and in gravity to those of other towns with populations equal in size.

The Alexandrians of today can be considered without doubt amongst the most hospitable people in the world: Galal el-Din ibn Mokram, 'Master of those who know by heart', would be surprised how he could have sung in former days:

He who descends at Alexandria receives as gift of hospitality only water, or the description of the Column el-Sauari. When one wishes to treat him well, they go so far as to give him fresh air, and point the Pharos out to him. They also describe the sea and its waves, adding also a description of the large Greek barques. Let not the guest have hope of receiving bread for in that place there is no man who can read that letter.

ALEXANDRIE - Jardin Français.

The French Garden.

Administrative Organisation. Alexandria is a Governorate. The Town has been administered since 1890 by a Municipal Council of twenty-eight members, eight of whom are nominated by the Government, six are ex-officio members, six are chosen by the general electors (i.e. citizens paying a rent of L.E. 75 per annum), three are elected by Importers, three by Exporters, and two by Landlords (house-owners). More than three members of the same nationality cannot be elected. The Governor of Alexandria is President of the Council. The members are divided into committees to supervise the different services.

The Council chooses a Delegation which is its permanent administrative and executive body. The Delegation is composed of seven members besides the Vice-President of the Council, who is a member by right, and who presides over it. The direction and supervision of all the services are entrusted to a Director-General who, without having a vote, attends the meetings of the Council, of the Delegation, and of the Committees. The Municipal Service comprises the following branches: 1. Administration and Legal, 2. Receipts, 3. Technical, 4. Scavenging, 5. Parks and Plantations, 6. Sanitary, 7. Veterinary, 8. Archaeological, 9. Library, 10. Fire Brigade. At the end of each year the Administration publishes a volume of the reports of the Heads of the Departments on the progress of the various services.

In spite of the tendency of the Government to centralise in Cairo the direction of all branches of Administration, Alexandria still remains the seat of the Mixed Court of Appeal, Customs, Ports and Lighthouses, the Marine, Sanitary, and Quarantine Council, and the Post Office. For the Administration of Public Security, and for the proper control of other public services which do not depend on the Municipality, the town and its suburbs form what is called a Governorate. The Governor, who is at the same time (as we have already remarked) President, by right, of the Municipal Council, is the representative of the State in Alexandria. He is assisted by a Sub-Governor, and by the Commandant of the Alexandria City Police. Moreover the Ministers, the Administration of the Caisse de la Dette Publique, and the English Diplomatic Agency reside in Alexandria during the summer months.

The family of the Sultan spend a certain portion of the year at their residence, the Palace of Ras el-Tin.

Climate, Hygiene, Comfort. In antiquity Diodorus, Strabo, Ammianus Marcellinius, Quintus-Curtius, Celsus and Pliny praised the salubrity of the Alexandrian climate. This salubrity caused the city to be frequented by valetudinarians, just as certain exceptionally sheltered towns on the coast of the Mediterranean are frequented at the present day. Every year brought a swarm of aristocratic patients to Alexandria to be treated for consumption. "At Alexandria", says Strabo, "the waters of the Nile begin to rise at the beginning of the summer, fill up the basin of the lake, and leave no marshy part exposed from which dangerous exhalations might arise. At this same time of year the Etesian winds blow from the North, after having crossed a great expanse of sea: therefore the summer is a very agreable season for the Alexandrians."

The fame of the salubrity of Alexandria was very great even at the time of the Arab historian Makrizi (1441). "Those who busy themselves with cosmography, the description of countries, the arrangement of climates and of regions, affirm that in no other country of the world, the years of men are as long as at Marabut, in the district of Alexandria, and at Wadi Farganah."

Nowadays, the climate has a rather bad reputation, but one ought not to lose sight of the fact that even if the north and north-westerly winds dominate here, and if during the months from August to November one of its essential characteristics is great humidity, yet these

The palace of Count Zizinia on Place des Consuls (Mohamed Ali Square), 1862. Destroyed by British bombardment in 1882, it was reputed to have had a library of 60,000 volumes and many valuable works of art.

Place des Consuls (Mohamed Ali Square).

Place des Consuls (Mohamed Ali Square).

inconveniences are mitigated by advantages of capital importance. We refer to its great thermal stability, to the incomparable purity of the air, and to the breeze which, during the summer, blows continually from three o'clock in the afternoon. From meteorological observations of several years it is seen that the minimum temperature gives an average of 16 degrees Centigrade, the maximum temperature an average of 24 degrees. Rarely, even during the hottest months, does the temperature exceed 31–32 degrees. It rains very little in Alexandria and almost exclusively in November, December, January and February (from 4 to 7 centimetres total rainfall every month); for the rest of the year only a few drops fall.

The *Khamsin* is a very hot wind from the desert, of which one is apt to form an exaggerated idea. It generally blows for two or three consecutive days at a time, and that during the fifty days before the Summer Solstice.

Since the Water Company has put new filters into use, the water that is distributed does not present the least danger; on the contrary it is so pure that it can bear comparison with the best drinking water known. The Municipality makes constant efforts to ameliorate in an effective manner the hygienic conditions of the town. Many sanitary works have been carried out, many insanitary establishments destroyed, a rigorous surveillance is exercised over every infectious malady, which is combated mercilessly, so that the percentage of mortality is constantly diminishing. During the last years it has been steadily on the decrease: in 1912 it was reduced to 33.6% for natives, and 12.8% for foreigners.

Alexandria offers visitors pleasant walks and drives, as picturesque as they are varied, and also the attractions of a great town, such as horse racing, sports, theatres, concerts and lectures. There are likewise first-class hotels.

Public Buildings. It can hardly be affirmed that our engineers and our modern architects have equalled Dinocrates or his collaborators and successors in making Alexandria a town of architectural beauty. Indeed we are almost obliged to confess that the greater number of public and private buildings are of mediocre taste. Some isolated attempts foretell that the sentiment of what is beautiful is beginning to penetrate even the least cultivated minds. Besides the buildings mentioned on a later page, we should like to draw attention to the Banco di Roma, at the corner of Rue Cherif Pacha and Rue Toussoun Pacha; the Consulates of France and Italy on the New Quay, in the Eastern Harbour; the Lycée Français at Chatby; the Italian School in the rue du 1er Khedive; the Egyptian Secondary School at Moharrem Bey. The new public parks and the broad quay in the Eastern Harbour have certainly contributed to heighten the beauty of the town.

The suburb of Ramleh too, although it is being developed too rapidly and on no preconceived plan, possesses several handsome private properties surrounded by superb gardens. Numerous villas are scattered about under the palm trees, a picturesque sight. The Route de la Corniche, which has been proposed and part of which has already been constructed between Silsileh (Cape Lochias) and San Stefano, will follow the shore of the Mediterranean for a distance of eight kilometres and will form one of the most beautiful promenades in the world.

Commerce. The commerce of the Port of Alexandria has increased to astonishing proportions in the course of these last years. In 1912 statistics furnished us with the following details. Steamers arrived: 1,927, departed 1,933, total 3,860. Tonnage net of the total register of steamers, arrivals and departures: 6,971,247 tons. Goods: arrived 2,660,170 tons, left 1,417,029, that is to say a total of 4,077,199 tons. Passengers: 182,782. Sailing-ships: 749 arrivals, 754 departures, total 1,503; register of total tonnage for sailing-ships, arrivals and departures: 184,065 tons. Goods imported: 68,917 tons, exported 37,353, total 106,270 tons. Value of the cotton crop: L.E. 26,507,955.

Place des Consuls (Mohamed Ali Square).

This is the highest figure that has ever been reached. This enormous movement in commerce necessitates each day new works of improvement in the port: new quays are constructed, the outer port is being enlarged, and lastly a new channel has been made, inaugurated 1908, navigable at all times and for ships of the highest tonnage, for their arrival as well as departure.

Intellectual Life. Besides numerous primary and secondary schools of different nationalities and some technical schools, Alexandria possesses a free popular University where modern languages are taught, and series of lectures are given on all subjects likely to interest the mind and develop a higher culture. A well frequented conservatoire tries successfully to propagate a taste for music among the people. The town can pride herself on possessing a library of about 25,000 volumes, an archaeological museum whose importance increases each day, and a gallery of pictures recently given to the town by the late M. Friedheim. An Archaeological Society, counting about 130 members, does much to awaken the interest of Alexandrians in the past glory of their city. This Society has carried out excavations, held conferences, organised excursions, and publishes an Archaeological Bulletin. A Society of Natural Science founded in 1908, draws together a certain number of amateurs and scholars. By the initiative and under the patronage of His Highness Sultan Fouad I, a large Institute of Hydrobiology is being founded, which promises to become the most important institution of this nature in the Mediterranean. Besides the numerous daily political papers edited in all languages, there are scientific and literary reviews published every month or every other month. Sometimes these do not last longer than the roses, but the frequency of their appearance is perhaps a proof that they supply an intellectual need felt by the population.

A visit to the Modern Town. The centre of the modern town is formed by a vast rectangular square (about 450 metres long, and 100 metres wide) which bears the name of the founder of the prosperity of Alexandria, the great Mohamed Ali. In the middle of the square is a monument that the town has erected to his memory. This beautiful bronze equestrian statue is signed by Jacquemart and was cast in Paris; the base is of Carrara marble. To the west of the square are found the so-called Midan quarter (Arab Bazaar) and Rue Franque which leads to the harbour, to the Bay of Anfouchy, to the ancient cemetery of the same name and to the Palace of Ras el-Tin, the summer residence of the Sultan. The visitor is advised to follow the fine road along the quay in the Eastern Harbour to Anfouchy Bay and continue the promenade as far as the Sailing Club, where a magnificent view of the harbour can be obtained.

A few hundred metres down Rue Franque, which starts on the west side of Mohamed Ali square, the Ibrahim Terbana Mosque is seen, built in 1685 (Christian era) with materials belonging to monuments of the Graeco-Roman epoch.

"This building," says M. Herz Pacha, "is a large rectangular, massive structure, plastered and whitewashed and having along one of its longitudinal fronts small shops with awnings made of matting: there is a school above and an exterior gallery formed of small columns supporting horseshoe-shaped arches and provided with a wooden balustrade. The edifice is surmounted by a minaret with blunted corners, terminating in a hexagonal gallery, from which rises a cylindrical column surmounted by a bulb. The narrow and plainly ornamented door is near the corner of this facade, and there is a stairway of five or six steps. Originally this door was handsomely decorated, but it is now entirely defaced. In the interior, the walls and the prayer niches are ornamented with faience tiles, with all sorts of geometrical forms, of the same type as those found at Rosetta."

The Mosque Abdel Baki el-Churbagi, situated at the beginning of Rue Ras el-Tin, was constructed in 1757. There is a large open gallery on the facade.

The Bourse on Mohamed Ali Square.

Further on, on the right of Rue Ras el-Tin, between it and the quays, is seen the Mosque of Sidi Aboul Abbas el-Mursi, to which access is given by the *midan* of the same name. This mosque is the most venerated in the town because it bears the name and shelters the tomb of a famous learned man who died in 686 of the Hegira (1287–88). Nothing now remains of the original mosque. The present edifice was erected in 1180 of the Hegira (1766–67) by pious Maghribians.

On the south side of Mohamed Ali Square, attention should be drawn to the Palace of Justice, some handsome edifices such as that of M. Primi, the Ottoman Bank Buildings, the Menasce Gallery and finally the palace of Prince Ibrahim in the Moorish style. The interminable Rue des Soeurs which starts on this side of the square, and down the whole length of which a double tram line is laid, leads to Minet el-Bassal (where are the great depots of cotton, wood and cereals), to the goods station at Gabbari, and to the suburb of Mex (in front of the Labbane Police Station a line branches off and goes to the Harbour). To the south-east of this street, a few paces from Mohamed Ali square, there is the square of St. Catherine's Church. Not far from this is the Patriarchal Greek Orthodox Church, and the seat of the Catholic Latin Archbishop. On the north side of Mohamed Ali square, Monferrato Buildings should be noticed, and a little further on, close to Rue de la Poste, Saint Mark's Buildings. In the garden surrounding St. Mark's Church, which adjoins St. Mark's Buildings, there is a bust of General Earle, killed at Kirbekan, fighting against the Dervishes, in 1885. The Bourse, built according to the plans of the architect Mancini, is between Rue Cherif Pacha and Rue Tewfik, and occupies the whole of the east side of the square.

There are some remarkable buildings in Rue Cherif Pacha, the ground floors of which are taken up by rich and elegant shops and numerous offices of banking or commercial companies. When the foundations were laid for the houses on each side of the street, ruins of several monuments of the ancient town were found, but unfortunately they were demolished or buried for good.

Rue Cherif Pacha is crossed halfway down by Rue Sesostris, a fine street with handsome shops. Rue Toussoun Pacha also opens out of Rue Cherif Pacha, and in it are situated the Banco di Roma, the National Bank, the Cassa di Sconto and the Land Bank. The handsome and effective building of the Banco di Roma is an imitation on a small scale of the celebrated Palazzo Farnese, which is considered one of the master pieces of sixteenth century architecture in Rome.

There are crossroads at the extremity of Rue Cherif Pacha. The street facing us is the Rue de la Gare du Caire, which also leads to the Moharrem Bey quarter and to the Mahmoudieh Canal. The street to the right is the Rue Sidi Metwalli, and that to the left Rue Sultan Fouad I.

These two last streets follow very closely the longitudinal avenue of ancient days — the Canopic Street — which was terminated by the Gate of the Moon at the west and the Gate of the Sun at the east. When digging the foundations of the Bourse Toussoun (Cook's Office) in 1886, the ruins of a Graeco-Egyptian temple dedicated to Osorapis and to Isis, to King Ptolemy Philopater and to his wife Arsinoe were found. If one wishes to visit the so-called Pompey's Pillar (Serapeum) and the Catacombs of Kom el-Chogafa, the streets to be taken are Rue Sidi Metwalli, Salah el-Din, Premier Khedive, and Pompey's Pillar. Rue Nabi Daniel is 100 metres down Rue Rosette. It is believed that the Mosque Nabi Daniel, in front of the former French Consulate, at the foot of Kom-el-Demas, covers the place where there used to be, and in the opinion of many still should be, the Tomb of Alexander the Great. The small hill that rises to the right of Rue Fouad I, beyond Kom el-Demas, is known by the name of Kom el-Dikka, and corresponds to the Paneum of ancient days; this was a monumental

St. Mark's Church on Mohamed Ali Square. Postcard dated 1906.

park. At the foot of Kom el-Demas at the side of Rue Fouad I, in digging the foundations of the Boustros Building, no. 28, a colossal statue of Hercules was found, which is now in the museum. Also, in digging the foundations of the Lifonti Building, a large base bearing the name of the Emperor Valentinianus was found; and under the foundations of the Zizinia Theatre a fine statue of Marcus Aurelius came to light as well as other marble statues. There is no doubt that this spot was one of the most important centres of the ancient town. Canopic Street was flanked along its whole length by handsome porticoes, temples and rich palaces, of which the columns and debris are now hidden under the present buildings.

Amongst the modern edifices should be mentioned the New Khedivial Hotel and the charming Palace of Count Zogheb, now the seat of the Native Tribunal; further on there is the Municipality, and to the north of it the museum, in the street of the same name.

If the visitor continues to the end of Rue Fouad I, and turns towards the left, following the tram lines, the public gardens of Rue Sultan Hussein are reached. In the lower part of the gardens, the fine three-storied cistern of el-Nabih can be examined. In these same gardens, a monument has been erected in honour of Nubar Pacha, Minister of Foreign Affairs under the Khedive Ismail, President of the Council of Ministers, and Minister of the Interior under Tewfik. He contributed greatly to the Europeanising of Egypt. By the care of the late Dr. Schiess Pacha, a large column of pink Aswan granite has been set up in Saïd Square. The column was found in a neighbouring property belonging to the Barons Menasce. It and the capital of greenish granite which surmounts must have belonged to a great building in the royal quarter of the town during the Ptolemaic period. At the sides of the base there are two statues of Sekhmet (goddess of war) with a lioness head. The small hill on which are the Government Hospital buildings and garden probably covers ruins of important Ptolemaic and Roman buildings,

perhaps even the Theatre. The garden should be visited, because an ancient sarcophagus can be seen there made of granite flanked by two beautiful columns with Christian reliefs, which, it seems, came from the ancient Church of Theonas. The sarcophagus as well and the columns were placed there through the care of the former Director of the Native Hospital, Dr. Schiess Pacha, who is interred there. He also set up the column in white marble seen at the summit of the hill, in memory of Queen Victoria's Jubilee. From this same spot there is a superb view over the sea and the town. On turning to the north there are the various suburbs of Ramleh; to the left and behind the spectator, the whole town from Fouad I Gate to Mex; in front the sea, an immense expanse of striking beauty, under the intense light of a sky that is always blue; at the foot of the hill is the New Quay, a colossal work which has enriched the town by a splendid promenade, to be ornamented later on with palaces, edifices and statues which, let us hope, will constitute a worthy homage to art and to aesthetics.

The New Quay surrounds the ancient harbour (Portus Magnus) from Cape Lochias (north-east) to the Pharos (north-west: Fort Kait Bey), and we know that this spot was covered with the marvellous constructions that were the pride of ancient Alexandria.

Descending by the Boulevard Sultan Hussein and following it, Rue Missalla (the Street of the Obelisk) is reached. This street took its name from the obelisks known by the name of Cleopatra's Needles, which stood at the end of it between the Ramleh Tram Station and the present house of Yehia Pacha. These obelisks, one of which was standing and the other lying on the ground, marked the entrance or one of the entrances to the Caesareum or Sebasteion, a vast and celebrated temple dedicated to the worship of the Emperors. One of these obelisks was ceded to the United States and at the present time decorates a square in New York; the other was sent to London where it was set up on the Thames Embankment.

Cherif Pasha Street.

Rue Missalla opens, on the left, on to the Boulevard de Ramleh where there are many noticeable buildings. This street is always very full of life because it leads to the Terminus, beyond which are the rich suburbs that lie to the east of the town. The Boulevard de Ramleh comes to an end not far from Mohamed Ali square whence we started.

Ramleh. The Arab signification of the word Ramleh is "sand" or "desert", but at Alexandria it has a broader meaning and is applied to the collection of suburbs all along the eastern coast from Ibrahimieh to the Khediva-Mother's Palace. These suburbs stand on a narrow line of sandy hills between the sea, Hadra Lake and the Mahmoudieh Canal. Ramleh's origin is recent. Half a century ago it was *ramleh*, sand, in the true meaning of the word, because except for a few groups of poor little Arab houses and Bedouin tents there was not a single European house. The constant development of these suburbs has been surprisingly rapid. Several factors may have contributed to this: a railway line, constructed about forty years ago, and transformed recently (1904) into an electric tram line; the dryness of the climate in contrast with the dampness of the town; and finally the extraordinary, if somewhat unsound, outburst of general prosperity in Egypt before the financial crisis which supervened in 1907–8. A stay in Ramleh is not only very healthy but very pleasant too, thanks to the proximity of the beach, of the gardens which surround the greater number of the houses, and of the many groups of date palms. It might be said that this suburb realises one's ideal of a garden city.

Ramleh, today, numbers about 40,000 inhabitants. If it had not a very great population during the Ptolemaic epoch, it was thickly populated during the Roman epoch, from the days of Octavius Augustus. This suburb was first called Juliopolis and later on Nicopolis. Let the visitor take the tram at the Ramleh Station and ride on the tram top if there is not too much wind. Just before arriving at the station of the so-called Caesar's Camp we see the modern European cemeteries to the right, and on the esplanade to the left, the Necropolis of Chatby, so called, one of the most ancient cemeteries in Alexandria. It was explored by the museum in 1904–1905. After Camp Caesar Station come those of Ibrahimieh, of the Sporting Club (see to the right, the race course, polo, lawn tennis, golf ground), of Cleopatra, of Sidi-Gaber, of Moustapha Pacha (military barracks, close to the old Roman Camp), of Bulkeley, Fleming, Bacos, Seffer (Hotel Beau Sejour), Schutz (Hotel de Plaisance), San Stefano (Hotel Casino, bathing establishment; and music every day in the summer), Beau-Rivage (hotel; skating rink), Palace Station, to Victoria College.

This promenade from Alexandria to San Stefano can also be made by carriage, leaving the town by Rue Fouad I and following a road parallel to the tramway. This road is bordered by gardens and villas. During the whole year, in the afternoons, there is a constant going and coming of carriages, motor cars, horses and bicycles. In front of Ibrahimieh, to the right of the road, there is the village of Hadra, near the site of the suburb Eleusis of ancient days. The last vestiges of the celebrated temple Telesterion, built by Ptolemy II, existed up to the middle of the nineteenth century, near Lake Hadra. It was there that the remains were discovered of the colossal statues of green granite of Anthony as Osiris (now in the museum courtyard) and of Cleopatra as Isis (now in Belgium, in the chateau of Baron de Warocqué).

Mahmoudieh Canal. A no less pleasant promenade is that to the Mahmoudieh Canal as far as the Nouzha Public Garden. A visit may also be paid a little further on to the Antoniadis Garden which encloses a hypogeum of the Roman epoch. A fine avenue leaves the Aboukir Road in front of the entrance to the European Cemeteries and leads to the Round Point (Water Company Offices). Thence other avenues separate and turn to the Mahmoudieh Canal, either through Moharrem Bey, or through Hadra (the journey there may be taken by Moharrem Bey and the return by Hadra).

Cherif Pasha Street.

The canal which today bears the name of Sultan Mahmoud was not made by Mohamed Ali. The founder of modern Alexandria confined himself to the repairing and cleaning of the canal which had existed since the foundation of the ancient town, and which branched off from the Canopic arm of the Nile at Chereum and Schedia (Kariun–Kom el-Gizeh) near Kafr el-Dawar. The bed of the new canal follows the line of the ancient bed from that place until some 100 metres from its end, where it abandons its old course to make a bend to the west of the goods railway station at Gabbari, thence discharging into the harbour.

Above Schedia, the Mahmoudieh follows the course of the Fouah Canal. Mohamed Ali spent 7.5 million francs on this work, and employed 250,000 workmen.

The canal is constantly used by boats with one or two immense white sails. When the breeze drops, these boats are towed by men who draw them with ropes. One might almost say that nothing on the canal for the last 20 or 23 centuries has been changed at all, and now and then our imagination might lead us to think that we were still living in that time so long gone by. The canal banks are shaded by gigantic trees, and the road along the bank passes in front of rich villas. The vast, calm expanse of Lake Mareotis, seen to its full extent, adds to the picturesqueness of this beautiful Egyptian landscape.

Nouzha Garden. It takes twenty minutes from the Round Point to arrive at Nouzha Garden, the property of the town. It comprises an area of about 7.5 acres; formerly arranged as a park by Khedive Ismail, it was afterwards abandoned, retaining only a vestige of its ancient splendour. The Municipality recently conceived the happy idea of rearranging it and restoring its former beauty. Tropical vegetation flourishes in all its richness, in the midst of a magnificently situated landscape; side by side with small plantations there are large spaces left free, reserved for gatherings of the "grown ups" as well as for the children's games; there is a bandstand; here and there shelters for picnic parties add western comforts to the suggestions of an Oriental landscape. (There is also a small zoological garden). From the highest point there is a very fine view over Hadra Lake, Ramleh promenade, and the suburbs of Ibrahimieh, Sidi Gaber, and San Stefano. In 1918, Mr. Antony J. Antoniadis made a gift to the town of his lordly domain known as Antoniadis Garden, which comprises gardens covering an area of about 40 feddans and a large villa. This domain adjoins the Nouzha Municipal Gardens. The magnificent park of the town has thus been considerably extended and forms a beautiful resort, worthy of a great metropolis.

Boulevard de Ramleh.

Alexandrie. La Bourse et la Rue Cherif Pascha.

The Bourse and Cherif Pasha Street.

Rue de la Gare de Ramleh.

Rue de la Poste.

Rue Rosette, the Municipality.

Rue du 1er Khedive.

Rue Porte Rosette.

Cook's Corner.

No. 49. Alexandrie. Le Palais de la Municipalité.

Khardiache F., Alexandrie.

The Municipality.

Rue Porte Rosette and the New Khedivial Hotel.

Rue Attarine with the Karakol (police station).

Place St. Catherine

A triangular green. Here is the traditional site of St. Catherine's martyrdom, whence she was transported to Mount Sinai by angels. But the legend only dates from the 9th century and it is unlikely that the saint ever existed. Franciscans settled here in the 15th century and built a church that has disappeared. In 1832 Mohamed Ali granted land to the Roman Catholics, and the present Cathedral Church of St. Catherine was begun. It fell down while it was being put up, but undeterred by the omen the builders persisted, and here is the result. Gaunt without and tawdry within, the Cathedral makes no attempt to commemorate the exquisite legend round which so much that is beautiful has gathered in the West; St. Catherine of Alexandria is without grace in her own city. The approach to the church has however a certain ecclesiastic calm.

E. M. Forster, *Alexandria: A History and a Guide*, 1922.

Vue générale d'Alexandrie de la place de l'Église et de l'Hôtel Abbat

Agopian, Alexandria, Egypt.

General view of St. Catherine Square and Hotel Abbat. Postcard dated 1901.

The Jews of Alexandria

The Jewish community had ancient roots in Egypt. Historically, it consisted mainly of Arabic-speaking Rabbanites and Karaites. The Rabbanites base their religion on the written Torah, the oral Torah, and the Rabbinic commentaries. The Karaites only accept the written Torah. There were Oriental Jews from North Africa, the Levant, Iraq and Yemen; Sephardim expelled from Spain and Portugal who had settled in Italy, around the Mediterranean and in the Ottoman Empire; and Ashkenazim who escaped Russian and East European pogroms and later the Nazis.

The 1927 census puts the number of Jews in Alexandria at around 25,000. In the 1930s, there were fifteen synagogues in Alexandria.

Jews first lived in the old Turkish quarters by the port—Haret el-Yahoud by the old fish market, where the two oldest synagogues were built, was poor. By 1900, affluent Jews had moved to Moharrem Bey, the upscale neighbourhood where they built their first hospital, several schools, and two synagogues, Green and Castro. They also lived in the fashionable Greek quarters and followed the city's expansion towards Ramleh.

The community had an upper crust of bankers, financiers, industrialists, entrepreneurs, developers; a middle class of professionals, merchants, and intellectuals; and a poor lower class of mainly Oriental Jews, who were close to Egyptians and lived in the old Turkish quarters, dependent on the community's charity.

from *Les Juifs d'Alexandrie*, Sandro Manzoni, Cahier nº 65, November 2011, *Amicale Alexandrie Hier et Aujourd'hui*.

12376. Zaoud-el-Mara, Jewish Quarters, Alexandria, Egypt.

Zaoud el-Mara, Jewish Quarters. Stereoscope dated 1898.

Alexandrie   Temple Israelite Elian Anabi

Grand Temple Eliahou Hanabi on Rue Nabi Daniel, first consecrated in 1354, reconstructed in 1850, enlarged in 1856 and 1935. It held the Community Council, the Rabbinical Court and the Civil Office.

Temple Green, built in 1901, Rue Moharram Bey.

The Graeco-Roman Museum

The question of founding a museum in Alexandria was first discussed in 1891. Previous to this, private collections had been made by Zizinia, Harris, Pugioli, Demetriou, but they had vanished, the contents being distributed far and wide in Europe and America. The collection of the Egyptian Institute, which was in the nature of a public collection, had been removed to Cairo, when the Institute migrated there. In spite of this dispersal of the older collections, there was still hope that with care a valuable museum might be organized in Alexandria.

The remarkable researches of Mahmud el-Falaki and the learned investigations of Nerutsos had shown clearly that if Alexandria could not give to archaeological science and art the immense wealth of monuments which her past glory led one to expect, yet she held beneath her soil many historically interesting ruins. The Government Antiquities Department was willing to help and promised that permission would be granted to excavate some other Graeco-Roman sites.

The idea of founding a museum, which originated with the Athenaeum Society, was well received by the press. The public, the Government and the Municipality showed considerable interest.

After some preliminary discussion, an agreement was reached and the following project was adopted. The Municipality would find the funds for the premises, the staff, the necessary excavations, and for the upkeep. The Government Antiquities Department agreed to exercise a scientific control, to send us some antiquities to start with, and gradually to transfer to the Alexandrian museum the greater part of its Graeco-Roman collection. Giuseppe Botti was appointed Director. In the *Rivista Egiziana*, the official journal of *The Athenaeum,* he had shown the importance, the necessity, and the possibility of the museum. Full of enthusiasm, he set to work to classify as far as possible the few antiquities which were handed over to him. The first premises were 4 or 5 rooms rented in a house in Rue Rosette. But these premises were soon found to be insufficient, and the Municipality decided to build a museum on the ground situated north of its offices. The new building was officially opened in 1895. It consisted of rooms 1-10, which were eventually to form the west wing of a rectangular edifice. In 1896, rooms 11 and 12 were built. In 1899, rooms 13 to 16 were added, and rooms 17 to 22 were opened in 1904. Additional accommodation is now badly needed. A project which I hope will soon be put into execution has been drawn up. It consists in the creation of a wing on the south side of the rectangle, joining up the existing eastern and western wings.

As was to be anticipated, the rapid accumulation of antiquities prevented for some time scientific classification and gave to the different sections the appearance of temporary depots. We have now tried to classify the collection more systematically: — *a*) Topography of Alexandria. *b*) Epigraphy and (provisionally) manuscripts. *c*) Egyptian antiquities. *d*) Products of Graeco-Roman art which reveal the influence of indigenous art and vice versa. *e*) Iconography. Small Sculptures. *f*) Sculptures. *g*) Architecture *h*) Ptolemaic and Roman Mummies. Funeral furniture. Products of industrial art. *i*) Objects obtained from systematic excavations, classified in topographical order. *j*) Numismatics. *k*) Christian antiquities.

E. Breccia, *Alexandrea Ad Ægyptum,* 1922.

MOYΣEION

Graeco-Roman Museum.

The Menasce or Khartoum Column

Named the Khartoum Column to commemorate the retaking of Khartoum by Lord Kitchener, it was first known as the Menasce Column when it was found nearby during excavations for the Menasce Jewish School. The column of red Aswan granite had been brought to Alexandria in Ptolemaic times.

The de Menasce family is a Sephardic family who arrived in Egypt during the eighteenth century. Yaqub Levi de Menasce (1807–1887) was born in Cairo and began his career as a money changer and gradually emerged as the private banker of Khedive Ismail. His banking and trading company, J. L. Menasce et Fils, had branches in Cairo, Alexandria, Marseille, Liverpool, London and Manchester, managed by his sons. In 1871, he moved permanently to Alexandria.

He was granted Hungarian citizenship and ennobled Baron de Menasce by Emperor Franz Joseph in 1876.

His son, Béhor Levi, continued in the family's financial enterprises, but his grandson, Jacques Béhor de Menasce (1850–1916), deserted banking in favour of the cotton and sugar businesses.

From 1890, Jacques served as the president of Alexandria's Jewish Community for twenty-five years. The family was well known for its philanthropy, and later generations were prominent in the arts.

Nubar Pasha

Nubar Pasha Nubarian (1825–1899) was born in Smyrna and educated in France and Switzerland.

When he completed his education, he was summoned to Egypt by his uncle Boghos Bey, Mohamed Ali's chief translator.

He seconded his uncle as Mohamed Ali's translator, then became translator to Ibrahim Pasha then his successor Abbas Pasha.

Abbas Pasha sent him on a mission to London to negotiate the railway contract then as chargé d'affaires in Vienna.

He then became secretary to Said Pasha, then chief translator to Khedive Ismail who appointed him Minister of Communications and Railway, Minister of Public Works, Minister of Foreign Affairs, Minister of Commerce, and twice Prime Minister, the second time by the British.

The Menasce or Khartoum Column.

Alexandrie. Colonne de Khartoum.

Menasce or Khartoum Column.

Alexandrie. Statue de Nubar Pacha et colonne de Khartoum.

4
ZAKAL

Statue of Nubar Pasha and the Menasce or Khartoum Column.

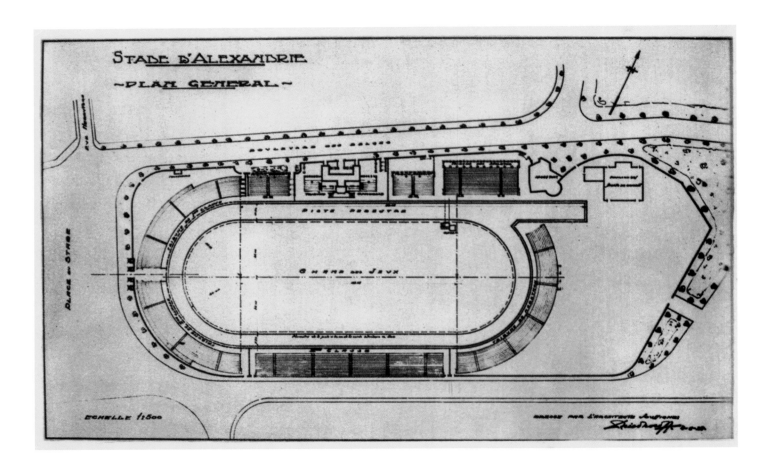

The Alexandria Stadium designed by W. Nicohosoff Bey, built by De Farro, 1927, and Cartareggia & Dentemaro, 1933.

Zizinia

Count Stefanos Zizinias, a pioneer in the cultural life of Alexandria, founded Theatre Zizinia, which for years was the centre of European cultural events in the city.

The theatre, inspired by Milan's Scala and designed by Pietro Avoscani, an Italian architect who had emigrated to Egypt, could accommodate 2,000 spectators.

Inaugurated in 1863, it became the city's most prestigious venue: Puccini attended a performance of his Madame Butterfly and Sarah Bernardt graced the stage. So did Mustafa Kamil Pasha, the nationalist leader, twice speak of Egyptian independence in 1896, the second address warmly received by an all-European audience.

The theatre was destroyed by fire in 1916/17.

Theatre Zizinia.

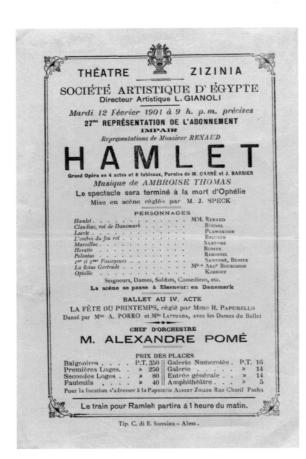

Programs of Theatre Zizinia.

Alhambra

In 1890, Salomon Conegliano acquired the *Théâtre de l'Exposition Egyptienne* on Rue de la Gare du Caire and renamed it Alhambra, competing with the more posh Zizinia.

Between 1901 and 1902, the old Alhambra also boasted a cinematographic hall in an annex.

In 1907, Conegliano and his son Bettino moved to a new location on Rue Safia Zaghloul Pacha (then Rue Missalaa) where they built the more modern, elegant New Alhambra, unrivalled in Alexandria after the Zizinia closed down.

Bettino became artisitic director after his father's death until he sold it in 1943, bringing renowned musical directors, tenors, orchestras, chamber music, ballet, dance and theatrical plays, whether French, Italian, English, Greek or Arabic.

Carlo Mieli, Alexandrie.

Alexandrie.   Jardin Alhambra, et Rue de la Gare du Caire.

The old Alhambra on Rue de la Gare du Caire.

The Mosque of Prophet Daniel

The Mosque of the Prophet [Nabi] Daniel which stands on the site of Alexander's tomb—the "Soma" where he and some of the Ptolemies lay, buried in the Macedonian fashion. The cellars have never been explored, and there is a gossipy story that Alexander still lies in one of them, intact: a dragoman from the Russian Consulate, probably a liar, said in 1850 that he saw through a hole in a wooden door "a human body in a sort of glass cage with a diadem on its head and half bowed on a sort of elevation or throne. A quantity of books or papyrus were scattered around." The present Mosque, though the chief in the city, is uninteresting; a paved approach, a white washed door, a great interior supported by four colonnades with slightly pointed arches. The praying niche faces south instead of the usual east. All has been mercilessly restored. Stairs lead down to two tombs, assigned to the Prophet Daniel and to the mythical Lukman the Wise; it is uncertain why or when such a pair visited our city. The tombs stand in a well-crypt of cruciform shape, above which is a chapel roofed by a dome and entered from the mosque through a door. Here and there some decorations struggle through the whitewash.

In a building to the right of the approach to the Mosque are the Tombs of the Khedivial Family, worth seeing for their queerness; there is nothing like them in Alexandria. The Mausoleum is cruciform, painted to imitate marble, and covered with Turkish carpets. Out of the carpet rise the tombs, of all sizes but of similar design, and all painted white and gold. A red tarboosh indicates a man, a crown with conventionalised hair a woman. The most important person buried here is Saïd Pacha—third tomb on the right. He was the son of Mohamed Ali and ruled Egypt 1854–1863. Mohamed Ali himself lies at Cairo.

E. M. Forster, *Alexandria: A History and a Guide*, 1922.

Mosque of Prophet [Nabi] Daniel.

Alexandrie. Fort de Kom-El-Dik.

Kom el Dekka. A hillock in the centre of Alexandria, today razed to the ground, once bore a fort built by the British as the town's main fortifications. It has also borne the names St Catherine Hill, Fort Napoleon and Fort Cafarelli.

Cairo Station, Alexandria's main railway station.

Kom el-Chougafa

The Catacombs of Kom el-Chogafa ("Hill of Tiles") are the most important in the city and unique anywhere: nothing quite like them has been discovered. They are unique both for their plan and for their decorations which so curiously blend classical and Egyptian designs; only in Alexandria could such a blend occur. Their size, their picturesque vistas, their eerie sculptures, are most impressive, especially on a first visit. Afterwards their spell fades for they are odd rather than beautiful, and they express religiosity rather than religion. Date—about the 2nd cent., A.D. when the old faiths began to merge and melt. Name of occupants—unknown. There is a theory that they began as a family vault which was developed by a burial syndicate. They were only discovered in 1900.

E. M. Forster, *Alexandria: A History and a Guide*, 1922.

187 - *Alexandrie* - *Kom-el-Chougafa*

Kom el-Chougafa.

Pompey's Column and Arab Cemetery

This column stands in its original position on the hill south of the outer wall (of the city of Alexandria) on the site of the Serapeum. The column stands on a pedestal over a foundation of smaller blocks held together with mortar and is crowned with a (pseudo-Corinthian) capital. One of the blocks bears a hieroglyphic inscription, indicating that probably all the foundation blocks originated from other monuments. The overall height of the monument is 32 metres, with the shaft of the column measuring 2.5 metres in diameter. According to the Greek inscription on its base, deciphered some few years ago, but since disappeared under more recent names, it was erected to honour Diocletian and the capture of Alexandria, in the year A.D. 296. The ruined remains of granite statues and columns are to be found on the same site. At the foot of this column the Arab Cemetery stretches away into the far distance in a very picturesque manner. The tombs, all facing towards Mecca, are generally surmounted by two small columns, the tallest of which is to be found beside the head, and is topped by a turban or a tarboush, depending on whether the deceased was Turkish or Arab. On the grandest of them are inscriptions recalling the memory of the deceased and calling for divine mercy upon him.

E. François-Levernay, *Directory of Egypt for the year 1872–1873.*

Pompey's Column and Arab Cemetery, circa 1890.

Cleopatra's Needles

A few steps from the Ramleh terminus in the New Port, there is still standing and fairly well preserved, one of the two monoliths known as Cleopatra's Needles; the other lies on the ground buried under rubble. According to Pliny, these obelisks, which from the time of Thutmose I (Thoutmôsis Misaphris, as he is described by Manetho) and were brought from Heliopolis to grace the entrance to the Caesareum or Palace of Caesar. They are made from syenite or pink granite. The one remaining upright stands at a height of 21 metres, on a base with sides measuring 2.5 m. It is covered in hieroglyphs which are poorly preserved, with the exception of those on the southwest side. The characters on this side form three columns. Reading the middle group from top to bottom: "Thutmose III, illustrious for having beaten the Hycks (Hyksos)".

E. François-Levernay, *Directory of Egypt for the year 1872–1873*.

Ramleh Station

The Ramleh terminus went through several stages, first as a railway station: construction from 1862 to 1868; stagnation from 1868 until the occupation in 1882; re-expansion after 1882 (a new station and an extension of the railroad); replacement in 1902/1903 of the engines by electric trams.

Ronny Van Pellecom, Peter Grech and Alain Stragier, *Alexandria Ramleh, Its Development and Postal History (1863–1929)*.

Cleopatra's Needle standing by Ramleh Station, circa 1856. One is now in Central Park, New York, and the other on the Embankment in London.

La Station du Chemin-de-fer de Ramleh   Alexandrie

48 Made for Pierre Agopian, Alexandria, Egypt.

Ramleh Railway Station, designed by 1883-4 by Antonio Lasciac, before the tramway.

118 ALEXANDRIA. -- *Bellevue Casino.* — LI.

Ramleh Station. The front became the entrance to the Bellevue Casino.

Ramleh Station with wooden tram stops.

1. ALEXANDRIE — Station of Ramleh

Ramleh Station with the wooden tram stops replaced by a stone building. Part of the Bellevue Casino appears in the background.

EDITION B. SIRVEN

ALEXANDRIA – RAMLEH STATION AND ITALIAN CONSULATE.

Ramleh Station and the Italian Consulate.

ALEXANDRIE - Station de Ramleh.

Ramleh Station in the 1920s.

Lingua Franca

Apart from the Arabic language spoken by the indigenous population and the Levantines, three main languages are spoken: French, Italian and Greek. The French language is predominant. It is the official language of government, used by public authorities and a large number of consulates. The official government gazette is written in the French language. Public announcements are in the French language which explains the widespread use of the French language on signs found in establishments and shops and on professional plaques.

E. François-Levernay, *Directory of Egypt for the year 1872–1873*.

113   ALEXANDRIA. — *Consulate of France.* — LL.

The French Consulate.

Cecil Hotel.

Iorio Palace Hotel, now Metropole Hotel.

The Corniche was built in stages, starting from Ras el-Tin Palace and the Eastern Harbour in 1901, ending in Montazah in 1934.

The Corniche, circa 1920.

The Greek Colony

Pandelis Glavanis

[The city of Alexander in the nineteenth and early twentieth century was home to the largest and most affluent Greek colony outside Greece. The Greek colony was the largest foreign community in Alexandria. Mohamed Ali, from Kavala in northern Greece, encouraged and offered refuge to Greeks from Ottoman persecution. As Ottoman subjects, Greeks were not protected by European consuls but they had access to a network of trade connections within Europe. That suited his expansion plans. Herewith are some prominent Greeks of Alexandria.]

Count Ioannis d'Anastasy (1765–1860?)

Ioannis Anastasios, one of the first Greek merchants to emigrate to Alexandria, was born in Thessaloniki. At an early age he emigrated to Malta where he engaged in trade. In 1805 he declared bankruptcy, settled 25% of his debt and emigrated to Egypt where he associated with the commercial activities of Mohamed Ali and his son Ibrahim Pasha. By 1820, he had become the Swedish Consul-General in Egypt with the title of count and changed his name.

He possessed a significant collection of Pharaonic antiquities. One particular sale to the British Museum, which included a papyrus written by an Egyptian officer on a military campaign to Syria during the sixth century B.C., brought him considerable financial rewards. In addition, d'Anastasy owned a substantial merchant fleet.

As one of the founders of the Greek community in Alexandria, his donations helped establish the first Greek school, hospital and church.

Michalis Tossitsas (1787–?)

Michalis Tossitsas was born in Metsovo, Epirus, northern Greece. His father was a wealthy fur merchant who moved to Thessaloniki (Salonika) in 1797. In 1806, Michalis became head of the family, managing his father's business with his three younger brothers. Tossitsas expanded his operations and established branches in Kavala, Malta and Livorno. In Kavala, he met Mohamed Ali and the two cooperated on a number of commercial enterprises. In 1818, Michalis sent his three brothers and sister to Egypt and concentrated on trade with Egypt. In 1820, his sister wrote to say that Mohamed Ali was well established in Egypt. Michalis wound up his business affairs and arrived in Alexandria in July 1820 where he was personally met by Mohamed Ali.

Mohamed Ali appointed Michalis Tossitsas overseer and manager of his estates, a substantial part of the most fertile land in Egypt. Tossitsas also advised Mohamed Ali on how agricultural products from State warehouses were to be sold to European merchants. Tossitsas became one of the most important and wealthy foreign merchants in Alexandria.

Tossitsas was appointed the first Greek Consul-General in Egypt in 1833, and elected first President of the Greek community in Alexandria in 1843.

Count Stefanos Zizinias (1805–1870)

Stefanos Zizinias was Michalis Tossitsas' nephew. Born in Chios, he emigrated to Alexandria following the massacre of Greeks by Ottomans at the start of the Greek Revolution in 1821.

Zizinias exported Egyptian products to European markets. He sent his four brothers to various European cities as his agents. The bulk of his trade was directed towards France and as his Ottoman citizenship was a hindrance, he applied for and received French citizenship as well as a decoration from the French government.

This proved beneficial to Egypt in 1825 when France prohibited the

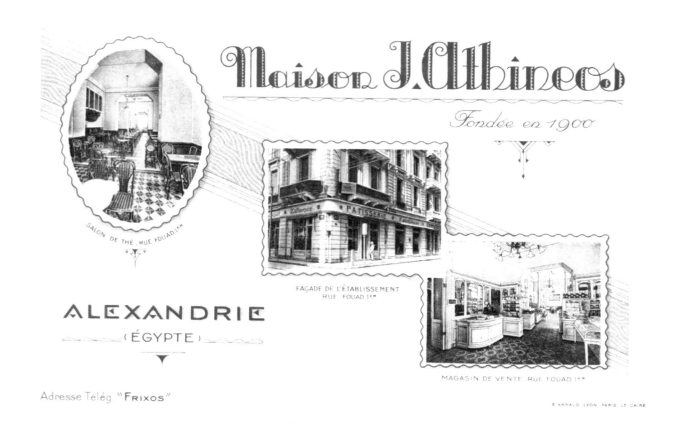

Maison J. Athineos

Fondée en 1900

SALON DE THÉ, RUE FOUAD Iᵉʳ

FAÇADE DE L'ÉTABLISSEMENT RUE FOUAD Iᵉʳ

ALEXANDRIE

(ÉGYPTE)

MAGASIN DE VENTE, RUE FOUAD Iᵉʳ

Adresse Télég "FRIXOS"

The Athineos tearoom off Ramleh Station, now the Trianon.

Toulouse shipyards from selling Mohamed Ali battleships. Zizinias, as a French citizen, purchased two battleships and donated them to the Egyptian navy. In compensation, Mohamed Ali gave Zizinias 15,625 acres of land just outside Alexandria. By the 1850s, this area called Ramleh had become an elite European suburb of Alexandria.

In 1840, Zizinias was awarded the title of Count by the monarch of Belgium and appointed Belgian Consul-General in Alexandria. When his uncle Tossitsas returned to Greece in 1854, he was elected President of the Greek community in Alexandria.

Stefanos Zizinias owned both agricultural land and urban real estate. His urban real estate which stretched for 15 kilometres east of Alexandria along the coast, from Ramleh to San Stefano, made him the largest landowner in Alexandria. Between them, Zizinias and Tossitsas then owned three-quarters of Alexandria and its environs. Zizinias also owned large estates of agricultural land on either side of the Mahmoudieh Canal.

Stefanos Zizinias established the first theatre in Alexandria, named Zizinia, which for several years was the focus of all European cultural events in the city.

The British bombardment in 1882 destroyed much of the family's property, including the palatial residence on Mohamed Ali Square which was reputed to have a library containing sixty thousand volumes and many valuable works of art. His son and heir, Menandros Zizinias, refused to sign the telegram sent by prominent Greeks of Alexandria congratulating Gladstone, so he did not receive any compensation. This spelled the end of the Zizinias prominence in Alexandria.

Petros Cavafy (1814–1870)

Petros Cavafy, father of well-known Greek poet Konstantinos Cavafy, was born to a prosperous merchant family in Istanbul and died poor in Alexandria. His father was in the cloth trade and resided in Manchester.

The first record of Petros Cavafy in Alexandria is his signature on a document dated May 30, 1844 when the Greek community in Alexandria established its own church independent of the Greek Orthodox Patriarch in Egypt.

He commuted between Alexandria and Istanbul until 1850 when he liquidated his affairs in Istanbul and settled in Alexandria.

In 1854, Petros Cavafy was elected Vice President of the Greek community in Alexandria.

By the early 1860s, the Cavafy firm was among the top ten foreign firms in Alexandria. Petros added cotton to his exports and established his first cotton gin in Kafr el-Zayyat in the Delta. By 1863, Petros Cavafy had branches in Alexandria, Kafr el-Zayyat, Cairo and Minya in Egypt and in London, Liverpool, Manchester and Marseille in Europe. That year, his son Konstantinos was born.

After Petros' death, his wife left to Manchester in 1872 and the Cavafy firm was dissolved in 1877. In 1880, Konstantinos Cavafy returned to Alexandria, where he worked at the Ministry of Irrigation to support himself.

Sinadinos

Konstantinos Sinadinos left Chios after the 1821 massacre. In 1830, he settled in Alexandria with his sons, Augustino and Ioannis

Augustino Sinadinos worked in the cotton trade and achieved enough respectability for one of his sons, Themistoklis, to marry, Eliza Rallis, the daughter of a wealthy Greek merchant in Alexandria. Themistoklis and Eliza had three daughters and one son, Augustino, who became a director of the Choremi-Benachi cotton exporting firm. Augustino was elected to the Alexandria Municipal Council, Vice-President of the

The Greek Tobacco Manufacturing Company was established by the Coutarelli brothers in 1890.

Greek Chamber of Commerce, President of the Alexandria Exporter's Association and a board member of several Anglo-Egyptian firms.

Ioannis Sinadinos focused on finance and banking. Along with the French Pastre brothers and Hambro of London, he established in 1864 the Anglo-Egyptian Bank, the first private commercial bank in Egypt. He established a second commercial bank with two other Greek financiers, Zervoudachis and Salvagos, and a merchant firm with Rallis. He had eight children, four of which were males: Konstantinos, Amvrosios, Mikes and Nikolaos.

Amvrosios became representative of the Rothschilds in Cairo and a close friend of Khedive Tewfik and Lord Cromer. Konstantinos and Mikes established the Societe Commercial d'Egypte, a leading merchant-finance firm in Alexandria.

Mikes Sinadinos was elected President of the Greek community in 1911 and remained in that position until his death in 1919.

Konstantinos Zervoudachis (1822–1895)

Konstantinos Zervoudachis was born in Chios. In 1835, he left for Alexandria where he sought the protection of a relative, Scaramanga, a prosperous merchant. With Scaramanga's assistance he embarked in commerce with his brother Nikolaos. Their efforts proved futile. In 1854, he married the sole heiress of Pantelis Mavrocordatos, of a wealthy and prominent Greek merchant family in Istanbul. In 1856, Zervoudachis established his own cotton trade firm in Kafr el-Zayyat.

By the end of the 1870s, Zervoudachis had become an important cotton exporter in Alexandria but failed to break into the closely knit social group of the city's prominent Greeks. He associated with newcomers such as Salvagos and Benachi who brought him close to British economic interests in Egypt. He was rewarded with a knighthood from Queen Victoria in 1882 and the wrath of the anti-British Greek press in Alexandria. As Sir Konstantinos Zervoudachis, he signed the telegram congratulating Gladstone in 1882 for occupying Egypt.

With British occupation, Sir Konstantinos Zervoudachis was elected Vice-President of the Greek community in Alexandria in 1885. His social status was confirmed by the fact that Khedive Tewfik, Lord Cromer and Sir Elwin Palmer sent messages of condolences when he died.

George, his eldest son, continued the family business, Zervoudachis and Sons: General Merchants and Bankers, developing the banking side. By the turn of the century it was a purely financial enterprise. George Zervoudachis was board member of the Bank of Egypt, Credit Union Fonciere, the Alexandria Water Company, and the Alexandria Tramway Company. He participated in a joint venture with British capital in metal exploration in Ethiopia. His only contribution to the Greek community in Alexandria was L.E. 15,000 towards the establishment of a Greek school in Chatby in 1907, named after his father.

With the 1907 financial crisis in Egypt, the family firm went bankrupt. One of the brothers, Amvrose, committed suicide in 1911. George died a pauper in 1912. The only brother to survive the crisis was Emmanuil who had inherited his rich father-in-law, Dranet Pasha. Emmanuil's daughter inherited her grandfather's fortune and married an unknown, poor Cretan lawyer named Eleftherios Venizelos who became one of the most important prime ministers in twentieth-century Greece.

Theodoros Rallis (1824–1890)

Theodoros Rallis was born in Aidinio, Asia Minor. Educated in Smyrna, he arrived in Egypt with his three brothers in the early 1850s. They settled in the village of Talha, near Mansura in the Delta, and engaged in the cotton trade.

Christo Cassimis, 109 Rue Aboukir, Ibrahimieh. Founded 1882.

Theodoros Rallis introduced mechanical, steam-powered cotton gins to Egypt. He purchased twenty second-hand cotton gins from a British firm that had used them to process American cotton in England. Rallis adapted them to Egyptian long staple cotton. He also imported a cotton press and could send his customers in Alexandria cotton that had been ginned and pressed into bales ready for shipping. More cotton could be packed in a single cargo ship and Lancashire mills were spared the tiresome ginning. With the American Civil War and demand for Egyptian cotton, this proved invaluable.

With the introduction of cotton gins, cotton seeds were now available. Initially the cotton seeds were used as fuel, but soon Greek entrepreneurs extracted the oil and then manufactured products such as soap and edible oils.

By 1858, Rallis had become one of the wealthiest merchants in Alexandria where he had settled. In 1871, he was elected President of the Greek community until 1885 when he was forced to resign due to his anti-British attitude.

As President of the community he abolished school fees to ensure that Greek children went to Greek schools, and introduced business studies and three foreign languages, Arabic, English, and French, as compulsory subjects.

His brother Antonis had established the family firm, Rallis Brothers Company, in Britain. Theodoros did not have a male heir and his only daughter, Maria, married Amvrosios, son of Antonis Rallis.

Amvrosios Rallis was born in London in 1850 and graduated from King's College. He came to Alexandria where he married his cousin and worked for his father-in-law. When the latter died, Amvrosios inherited the whole family estate. Amvrosios was more British than Greek and chose the post of Vice-President of the Alexandria Municipal Council, Lord Cromer's brainchild, rather than the Greek community council. He remained Vice-President from 1896 to 1906, and was also elected President of the Alexandria Exporters Association from 1896 to 1907. This association, which was also British controlled, dominated all commercial transactions in the city. Amvrosios also became a member of the British Chamber of Commerce in Alexandria, rather than the Greek Chamber of Commerce which was established in 1901, and that same year dissolved the Rallis Brothers Company to take up a directorship at the Egyptian National Bank, a British institution.

Ioannis Choremi

Ioannis Choremi emigrated to Britain from Chios after the events of 1821. After working for a Greek merchant firm in Liverpool then a shipping company, in 1849, he started his own commerce and finance firm and partnered with Mr. Mellor, financing commercial activities between Britain and Egypt. In 1857, he emigrated to Alexandria to represent the Choremi-Mellor company and established a cotton exporting firm with an additional partner, Davis. The new firm, Choremi-Mellor-Davis & Co., became a leading cotton exporting firm, but Choremi was primarily interested in finance capital, devoting himself to establish the Alexandria Stock Exchange.

As the political situation deteriorated, his British partners left the firm. In 1876, Choremi went into partnership with Greek financier Benachi who had recently arrived in Alexandria from Manchester. The new firm, Choremi-Benachi Co., survived the turbulent years and by the end of the century was the top cotton exporting firm in Egypt. When he died in 1897, his son Konstantinos inherited the estate.

Konstantinos Choremi, British citizen born and educated in Liverpool, studied commerce in Marseille prior to joining his father in Alexandria where he was appointed co-director of Choremi-Benachi & Co. Upon his father's death, he became one of the wealthiest persons in

Alexandrie   Rue de l'Eglise Grecque

Rue de l'Eglise Grecque.

Alexandria and was elected President of the Alexandria General Produce Association from 1913 to 1930. He was also a prominent member of the board of the Egyptian Joint Cotton Company, the largest firm to finance cotton production and export in Egypt. His most important position was President of Minet el-Basal Cotton Exchange which he held for fifteen years.

George Averoff (1818–1899)

George Avierinos was born in Metsovo, Epirus in northern Greece in a prosperous family. With the start of the Greek Revolution in 1821, his five older brothers were forced to emigrate. The oldest went to Russia where he worked in Russo-Balkan trade, amassed a large fortune, and changed his name to Averoff. The rest of the family adopted the new name.

Three Averoff brothers settled in Cairo in the early 1830s and specialised in the transit trade with the Sudan. George Averoff, the youngest, joined his brothers in 1841. The three older brothers returned to Greece while George continued the family business without much success. During the 1850s, George Averoff started to work in the Egyptian cotton trade, but could not make much profit because of Alexandria merchants' monopoly. In 1865, at the height of the cotton boom, a severe cholera epidemic spread in Cairo and forced most of the foreign merchants to abandon their goods and flee to Alexandria. Averoff, who had no family to concern him, stayed behind and purchased large quantities of cotton from the fleeing merchants at low prices. At the end of the 1865 cotton season, he had made a profit of 120,000 Egyptian pounds. He moved to Alexandria and entered the elite social circles of Greek merchants.

Given the economic and political instability after Egypt's bankruptcy, the value of Egyptian government bonds and the price of real estate and agricultural land dropped dramatically. Averoff purchased all three: bonds in Alexandria's public amenities, agricultural land in the Delta and urban real estate in Alexandria. After the British military occupation of 1882, their value increased rapidly. By 1884, George Averoff was one of the wealthiest Greeks in Alexandria and was elected Vice-President of the Greek community. The following year, Rallis was forced to resign and Averoff became President.

In 1887, he donated 10,000 pounds sterling to pay half the debts incurred by the community in renovating property damaged in 1882. The Greek community had not received compensation from Britain, due to its anti-British attitude, and was compelled to borrow from commercial banks who were threatening to send the bailiffs. As President of the community, he formalised the independence of the Greek Orthodox Patriarchate in Alexandria from the Ottoman-controlled Greek Orthodox Patriarchate in Istanbul. Henceforth, the Alexandria Patriarch was appointed by the Alexandria Greek community.

In 1896, at the time of the first modern Olympics, Averoff paid the entire costs of constructing the marble stadium in Athens, thus ensuring that the games were held in Greece. Later he contributed 20,000 pounds sterling to the transformation of the engineering school that had been established by Michalis Tossitsas into the Metsovion Polytechnic, and it remains a leading institution of higher education in Greece. Averoff also established a military academy and an agricultural school in Larissa, northern Greece, and donated 56,000 pounds sterling for the construction of the first modern Greek battleship which was named after him. The *Averoff* was the flagship of the Greek fleet until the 1950s. Anchored in Faliron, near Athens, it is used for formal occasions by the Greek navy.

Konstantinos Salvagos (1845–1901)

Konstantinos Salvagos was born in Marseille where his father,

ALEXANDRIE. Asile des orphelins "Benaki".

The Benachi orphanage.

Michalis, was a prosperous merchant trading in Egyptian cotton. With the cotton boom, Konstantinos came to Alexandria in 1865 to establish a branch of Michalis Salvagos and Sons. Konstantinos quickly made large profits and established his own firm, K M Salvagos and Co. Though he continued to trade in cotton, he was primarily concerned with finance. The enterprises he founded, such as the National Bank of Egypt (established initially in his offices), the Alexandria Water Company, the Alexandria Ramleh Railway Company Limited, the Societe Anonyme du Behera, the Filature Nationale d'Egypte, were controlled by British capital.

He was elected second Vice-President, with Averoff, of the Greek community in 1884, and became President in 1900. His wife and son established the Salvagos School for Commerce in his memory in 1907, at the cost of L.E. 16,500.

His son, Mikes Salvagos, followed in his father's footsteps and expanded the family financial enterprises which permitted him to occupy several prestigious social positions in the city such as President of the Mohamed Ali Club, Vice-President of the Egyptian Industrialists Association and member of the Higher Economic Council of the Egyptian State. All three organisations were pro-British, established after 1882. He was also Vice-President of the Gabbari Land Company and the Societe Anonyme de Nettoyage et Pressage de Cotton, and a member of the board of the National Bank of Egypt, the National Insurance Company of Egypt and the Bank of Athens. Except for the last, all the other enterprises were British controlled. The capital for the Bank of Athens had been raised by prosperous Greeks in Alexandria.

Mikes Salvagos was elected Vice-President of the Greek community in 1911. In 1919, he became President, a position he occupied until 1944 when he resigned.

Emmanuil Benachi (1843–1929)

Emmanuil Benachi was born on the island of Sires where he received his primary education. In England, he completed a year and a half of secondary studies. In 1865, he emigrated to Egypt and worked as an agent for a Greek firm purchasing cotton in the villages. By 1868, he and his brother, Loukas, had established their cotton exporting firm in Alexandria.

His fate changed in 1870 when he married Virginia, the younger sister of Ioannis Choremi, and was appointed a director in the Choremi-Davis-Nellor and Co. firm. He was sent to Liverpool to establish a branch of the firm. In 1876, after Davis and Mellor had left the firm, he returned to Alexandria as an equal partner in a new firm now called Choremi-Benachi and Co. This guaranteed his status in the city and prominence among Greek merchants and financiers. He was appointed to the Comité d'Elite in 1882, a civil organisation established by the British military to assist them in administering Alexandria after the occupation. When Lord Cromer established the Municipal Council, he was elected to its governing board.

Benachi was President of the Mohamed Ali Club, a pro-British socio-political association; member of the executive committee of the Khedive's Agricultural Society, which considered all matters pertaining to the cultivation of cotton; and member of the governing council of the Egyptian Cotton-Ginners Company Limited, responsible for regulating all cotton ginning enterprises in Egypt. In addition to being a partner in the largest cotton-exporting firm in Alexandria, Benachi was an important financier, on the board of various British-controlled enterprises such as the National Bank of Egypt, the National Insurance Company of Egypt and the Egyptian Salt and Soda Company.

He was elected Vice-President of the Greek community, with Averoff, in 1884. In 1901, he became President. As President, he donated 88,000

The Greek School.

square yards of urban real estate where he constructed an orphanage and a public kitchen for the poor Greeks of Alexandria. Inaugurated in 1909 and 1908 respectively, both institutions were administered by his wife, Virginia, who was also the director of a number of other charities in the city. He was instrumental in establishing the Greek Chamber of Commerce in Alexandria in 1901 and became its first President. It permitted the Greek government and British authorities in Egypt to influence and control Greek merchants, bankers and financiers in Alexandria. This was one of the principal reasons why Venizelos, the Greek Prime Minister, appointed him Minister of Agriculture and Trade in 1911. Venizelos was consolidating his relations with Britain to counteract the pro-German Greek Royal family. Benachi was also given the task of introducing cotton cultivation to Greece, which Venizelos hoped would revitalise Greek agriculture and provide foreign currency.

Benachi remained in the Greek cabinet until Venizelos lost the elections in 1915. He was then elected Mayor of Athens as an independent. When he died in 1929, he was succeeded by five children. His three daughters married the sons of Choremi, Salvagos and Deltas, all wealthy Greeks from Alexandria. His older son, Alexander, died at a young age. Antonis inherited the family fortune. His only public role was establishing the Greek Boy Scouts Association in Alexandria and Greece in 1924 and 1926 respectively.

ΕΛΛΗΝΙΚΟΣ ΑΘΛΗΤΙΚΟΣ ΟΜΙΛΟΣ ΙΒΡΑΗΜΙΑΣ

HELLENIC IBRAHIMIEH SPORTS CLUB

FONDÉ EN 1915

Enregistré auprès du Ministère des Affaires Sociales sub. No. 107.

102, Rue Memphis, 102

Téléphone No. 72822

ΙΔΡΥΘΕΙΣ ΤΩ 1915

ΕΓΚΡΙΣΙΣ ΑΙΓ. ΥΠΟΥΡΓΕΙΟΥ ΚΟΙΝ. ΠΡΟΝΟΙΑΣ ΑΡ. 107

نادى الابراهيمية اليونانى الرياضى

تأسس سنة ١٩١٥

مسجل لدى وزارة الشئون الاجتماعية تحت رقم ١٠٧

١٠٢ شارع ممفيس بالابراهيمية

تليفون ٧٢٨٢٢

Letterhead of the Hellenic Ibrahimieh Sports Club, an alternative club founded in 1915.

27

Alexandria - Lycée Français

The Lycée Français was established in 1909 by a group of parents who formed the *Société du lycée* and initially managed it with the *Mission laïque française* that subsequently took complete control.

COLLEGE SAINT - MARC

ALEXANDRIE (EGYPTE)

Collège Saint Marc, a boys' French Roman Catholic school in Chatby, was founded in 1928 by the Frères de La Salle and inaugurated by King Fuad. At the time, it was the largest educational institution in the Middle East.

Casa d'Italia Littorio Schools

The turning point in the city's fate, marking architectural morphology ever after, was the introduction of early modern international styles, experienced in the new concepts of the Italian Regie *Scuole Littorie* 1931–1933.

In 1929 the Italian government negotiated with the Municipality the purchase of approximately 27,700 m² for the building of a new school in Chatby, where a complex of educational facilities was in full development. The designs were entrusted to the prominent architect Clement Busiri Vici of Rome with experience in designing educational facilities for Italians in the colonies. Conceived in the Modern Style, the rational approaches of Busiri Vici reflected the image of a modern education, prompted by Italy's Fascist regime for the colonies in the diaspora. At a total cost of fifteen million Italian lira, the school was inaugurated in 1933.

The elevated school building was described as a modern castle, set in the middle of a carefully landscaped park. Symmetrical in composition, its buildings were grouped around a central piazza with side courts and terraced gardens. Central to the rational plan was the main auditorium around which were grouped two lateral pavilions, hosting the primary and secondary schools. Each pavilion, built on two floors, contained the classrooms and dormitories. Sport facilities featured as an integral part of the plan, emphasizing its importance in the new Fascist propaganda. In the conception of the plan, there is emphasis on simplicity and juxtaposition of form. Light was also a particular feature of the architecture, experienced in the imposing white mass that contrasted sharply with the scenic green-terraced landscaping. Environmental rationalism appeared in the treatment of shading devices, covered terraces and the treatment of transitional semi-open spaces, thereby linking outdoor and indoor activities in the educational facility.

The new look of the Casa d'Italia marked an undeterred route toward modernity, with every architect attempting its interpretation.

Mohamed Awad, *Italy in Alexandria: Influences on the Built Environment, 2008.*

ALEXANDRIA - The Italian School.

The Italian School.

El-Orwah el-Woska

El-Orwah el-Woska, a Muslim charitable society, was founded in 1892 to build vocational schools. Among its founders and advocates were the reformist Mufti Sheikh Mohamed Abdou and Mustafa Kamel, the nationalist leader. Between 1892-1907, it opened six girl schools in Alexandria with 531 pupils: 341 paying, 172 free, and 18 paying half fees. By 1912, it had 25 schools with 3603 pupils, of which 906 were girls.

El-Orwah el-Woska vocational school.

Camp de César Station.

Alexandrie (Egypte).   Ramleh Mazarita.

Mazarita, a corruption of Lazaret (quarantine), a quarantine station built by Mohamed Ali at the foot of Silsileh in 1831 and moved in 1882. In Arabic, it is called Lazarita, while in French it became Mazarita.

Alexandria's First Tramway 1898

Finally we have the tramway, and like Cairo, we have the electric tramway, and we can confirm that it was not without tribulations, irritating discussions and nuisances. But I imagine that when the director general M. Tivoli took his seat in the first car in front of H.H. the Khedive, he forgot the troubles of the previous days.

The presence of H.H. the Khedive was a great pleasure for all. Natives and Europeans were happy to see the young sovereign interested in the economic development of the country and all enterprises that augment the well-being of all. When His Highness arrived at St. Catherine Square at precisely half-past four, cheers and applause erupted as the tram carrying Khedive Abbas Helmi departed.

The invitations were few, given the strictly official nature of the event. The invitees were exclusively from the official world, the administration, and the press. Four gleaming cars, bedecked with flowers like newlyweds were at the guests' disposal. They were also decorated with Egyptian and French flags.

We shall not enumerate the personages we found happily grouped in each car. However, let us cite the members of the diplomatic and consular corps: Messers. Boutiron, the French minister, Pierre Girard, consul; de Coppet, vice-consul; Haggar, first dragoman of the French consulate; M. de Villiers, Russian consul; Cav. Burdese, vice-consul of Italy; Spagnolo, Spanish consul, etc. We also noted H.E. Ismail Sabri, governor of Alexandria, accompanied by H.E. the vice-governor and M. Beneducci, and H.E. Emin Pasha Fikri, the former governor and director of the Daira Sanieh.

The police under the orders of Major Cippolaro had taken the most comprehensive measures to maintain circulation. We hasten to add that this first day passed without incident. The personnel of the company were of the highest technical order.

The procession went to the slaughterhouse of Mex where it stopped then headed to Karmouz where the company plant is located. To M. Tivoli and the engineers Messers. Legrand and Daujat, the most hearty congratulations. We drank to the prosperity of the enterprise.

H.H. the Khedive graciously expressed his satisfaction to M. Tivoli, the Director General. He was most interested in the technical details proffered by M. Daujat, and he found the installation superior to that in Cairo.

H.E. Ghazi Moukhtar Pasha, Ottoman High Commissioner, went directly to the plant which he visited with H.H. the Khedive.

The ceremony ended at 6 o'clock and the electric cars returned the enchanted guests to St. Catherine Square. H.H. the Khedive left in a motorcar to the train-stand at Nouzha Station."

The collection then informs us that the following day trams transported an average of 60 persons per car—20 more than predicted—and that a pickpocket relieved his neighbour of his chain and gold watch.

Chronicles of the time specify that trams left every 10 minutes from different stations.

La Reforme, Golden Edition, 1945.

Share of the Belgian-owned Tramways d'Alexandrie, founded by Konstantinos Salvagos in 1897.

The Alexandria & Ramleh Railway Company

On 6 August 1860, the Egyptian government granted Sir Edward St. John, merchant, Britannic subject, permission to develop a railway connecting Alexandria and the suburb of Ramleh. The government reserved the right to withdraw the concession at any time while paying the concessionaire the price of the railway. At the time, the population of Ramleh did not exceed 500 inhabitants.

On 22 August 1860, Sir Edward asked the Egyptian Ministry of Foreign Affairs to authorise the founding of a stock company to execute his project at his expense. On 31 October 1860, the ministry approved his request, while declining all responsibility toward consequences and strictly adhering to the conditions of the 6 August 1860 agreement that held Sir Edward as the sole concessionaire responsible vis-à-vis the Egyptian government.

On 16 April 1862, the company Strada Ferrata Tra Alexandria e Ramleh was formed with a capital of 12,000 pounds divided into 1,200 shares. Sir Edward ceded the concession to the company against 30% of the profits for three years. The first rails were installed in September 1862 on the embankment of Cleopatra's Obelisk (the present Ramleh Station) with 1,200 workers on the job.

On 8 January 1863, the first public transport convoy departed Alexandria to Sheikh Ismail (currently Bulkeley Station) via Sidi Gaber Mosque. It comprised one first-class carriage, two second-class and one third-class, drawn by four horses. The price was 6 P.T. for first, 4 for second, and 2 for third class; the hours were: depart Alexandria at 8:30, 12:30 and 16:00, depart Ramleh at 9:30, 14:00 and 17:30.

On 23 August 1863, a locomotive replaced the horses. It had been imported in July 1863 and covered the distance in 20 minutes including stops at the stations.

On 3 October 1863, the board of directors issued annual subscription cards at 15 pounds for first class and 12 pounds for second.

On 25 January 1864, the first shareholders' general assembly was held. Total receipts were L.E. 4,421, total expenses were L.E. 3,033, after deducting a reserve of 10% and the 30% due to Sir Edward, which gave each share a return of 7.48%.

On 1 October 1865, the company concluded an agreement with the Postal Administration to transport mail from Alexandria to Ramleh.

On 28 June 1863, the company had been replaced by a new fixed capital company: the Alexandria and Ramleh Railway Co. Ltd.

On 1 April 1892, the company completed the installation of a new line between Sporting Station and Moustapha Pasha Station via the present Sidi Gaber Station, and stopped traffic on the old line passing by Sidi Gaber Mosque.

In 1897, the company began to double the route between Alexandria and Bulkeley. In 1898, the company purchased land to construct workshops and depots for its cars.

On 2 June 1898, the general assembly decided to replace the trains with electric locomotives.

In 1902, the city tramway company acquired the major part of the Alexandria and Ramleh Railway Co. Ltd.

On 25 January 1904, electrification was complete and electric locomotives were inaugurated. The lines had been extended to reach the Palace Station in 1904. The stretch from the Palace Station to the Mahmoudieh Station (now Victoria) was reserved for H.H. the ex-Khedive. The electric current was supplied by the Karmouz plant producing 6,000 volts transmitted by an underground cable to Chatby, then by an aerial cable to an intermediate plant at Bulkeley that transformed it to a steady 550 volts.

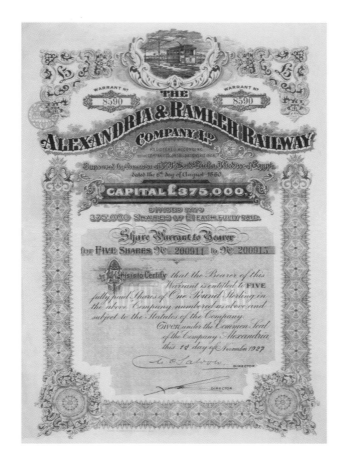

Share of the Alexandria & Ramleh Railway Company Ltd. dated November 1927. The British-owned company was founded in 1862 by Sinadinos, Zizinias and Zervoudachis.

On 17 March 1904, the company sold the land of the old Ramleh Station (where Cinema Strand stands) for L.E. 70,500 and built a permanent station between Mazarita and Cleopatra's obelisk which stood at the site of the actual station.

In 1909, the company inaugurated the stretch for public transport between the Palace and Mahmoudieh stations.

On 11 June 1914, the general assembly approved the board's decision of 10 April 1912 to replace the 1902 agreement for a final transfer between the city tram company and that of Ramleh, making the latter the sole concessionaire for the city network.

In 1915, the company built the Chatby electric power station with new diesel engines and transferred those of Bulkeley.

On 11 October 1919, the Council of Ministers ceded to the Alexandria Municipality the government's rights to withdraw its concession from the company.

In 1925, the company began enlarging its tramway yards in Moustapha Pasha. In 1928, the company restored the tram line between Sporting and Sidi Gaber stations which had been cut since 1892.

On 26 March 1928, the president of the Municipality issued a decree withdrawing the concession as of 1 January 1929. The decision was communicated to the government for its approval to pay the indemnity of taking over the company's network.

On 1 January 1929, the State Railways assumed the operation of the Ramleh network under the auspices of a governmental Council of Administration decreed by the Council of Ministers on 12 August 1928 and appointed a governmental director.

In November 1933, electric current was supplied to the generator station in Gabbari with supply from Chatby and Bulkeley stations which received it from the Karmouz plant.

On 31 January 1934, the Ramleh Electric Railway placed five autobuses in service between Mohamed Ali Square and Ramleh, alongside other autobus companies.

On 1 January 1937, the Ramleh Electric Railway acquired the rights for all autobus lines between Alexandria and Ramleh.

On 12 April 1939, the Council of Ministers decreed Ramleh Electric Company a legal entity designated Administration of Commuter Transport of Ramleh.

On 1 July 1939, this administration assumed control of autobus lines within the city.

La Reforme, Golden Edition, 1945.

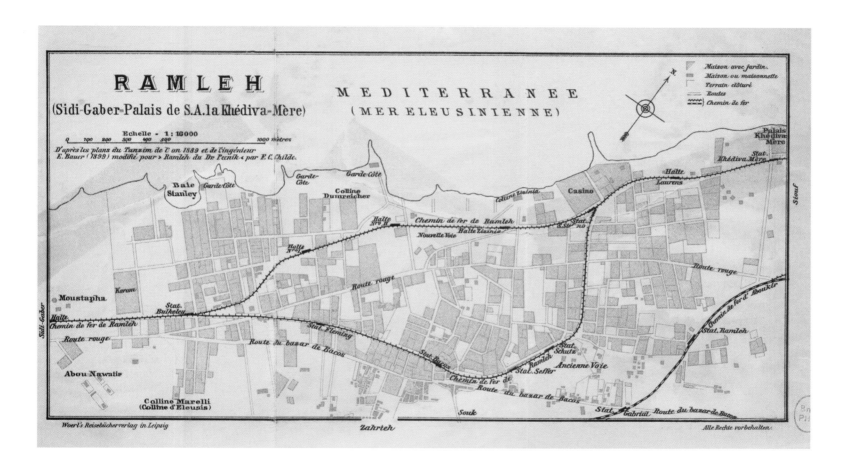

Map of the Alexandria & Ramleh Railway line from Sidi Gaber to H.H. the Khediva-Mother Palace.

Ramleh, The Eleusinian Riviera

Dr. Charles Pecnik

1901

The name *rámleh* in Frankish came from *raml*, which means "sand" in Arabic, because this station is located on an elevated strip of desert that extends from the Libyan Desert, from Mex and Alexandria, to Aboukir, then along the Mediterranean coast. Ramleh is not the name of a city, but of a small riviera whose coast is 4 or 5 hours long. Here and there are groups of villas which form the stations: Ibrahimieh, Sidi Gaber, Bulkeley, Fleming, Bacos, Seffer, Schutz, San Stefano, surroundings of the Khediva-Mother Palace, and the extension: Mandara, Montazah, Kharaba and Aboukir. Their collective name is Ramleh.

Some forty years ago, the region was a desert with no vegetation. At its limit, on the fertile countryside of the Nile, there were a few small Arab villages that can still be seen. But in the desert itself, there were only hunters' poor huts.

The place owes its rapid prosperity to a company that built some forty years ago (in 1863) a railway line from Alexandria to Ramleh.

Ramleh is crossed by the state railway, from Alexandria to Aboukir. The private company's railway does not go beyond the Khediva-Mother Palace where a Small Ramleh was formed, so to speak. A sandy land of about half an hour long separates Ramleh from Alexandria. The distance from Alexandria to the Small Ramleh is between 30 minutes to 2 hours depending on the station. There are trains every 15, 30 or 60 minutes. Consult the unpredictable timetable which is often changed. The price of the trip is 5 piastres in first class and 3 in third class. The price for a round trip is as little as 8 piastres in first and 5 in third. Soon all will change with the establishment of the electric traction. Ramleh has about 5,000 inhabitants; half are Europeans and the other half Arabs. The native language is Arabic. In the European colony, French dominates. Italian, Greek, English and a little German are spoken. The place is part of the governorate of Alexandria. Apart from the railroad that connects Alexandria to Ramleh, there is a nice tarmac road called the Red Road. The coastline from Alexandria to Aboukir goes from the southwest to the northeast. Not only is the region of Ramleh very beneficial, but also charming. Towards the north, the enchanted eye discovers the magnificent azure waters of the Mediterranean where the waves merge with the horizon. The coastline which is the Ramleh Desert has a slight formation of hills. The gray yellowish sand makes a superb light effect in the background. To the south-west, you can see Lake Mareotis (Marioût). Further away shines the sand of the Libyan Desert dunes. Towards the south, there is the everlasting greenery of the Nile's fertile country: gigantic groves of palm trees, which sometimes extend over several kilometres, plantations of fig trees, huge albizzias and sycamores, all in all, pleasant gardens and fields next to the sand.

Distances. An approximate estimation of distances to serve the sick, according to Professor Schwenninger's field cures (methodical steps). From Ramleh Station, with ordinary steps from one station to another (100 steps are approximately 1 minute):

Alexandria–Ibrahimieh: 3,600–3,800 steps, 37 minutes.
Ibrahimieh–Sporting Club: 850–900 steps, 8 and a half minutes.
Ibrahimieh–Sidi Gaber: 1850–1950 steps, 19 minutes.
Sidi Gaber–Bulkeley: 1950–2050 steps, 20 minutes.
Bulkeley–Fleming: 750–800 steps, 7 and a half minutes.
Fleming–Bacos: 800–850 steps, 8 minutes.
Bacos–Seffer: 420–460 steps, 4 and a half minutes.
Seffer–Schutz: 380–400 steps, 4 minutes.
Schutz–San Stefano: 780–820 steps, 8 minutes.

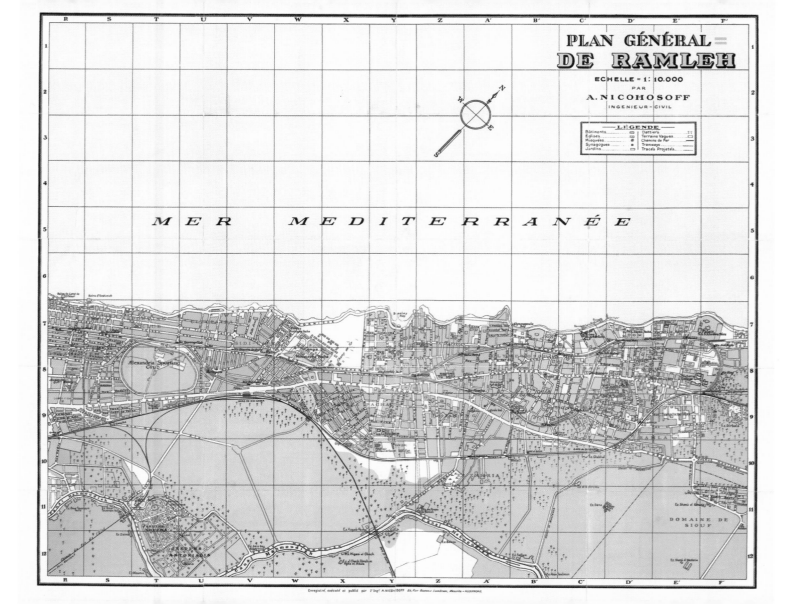

PLAN GÉNÉRAL = DE RAMLEH

ECHELLE = 1: 10.000
PAR
A. NICOHOSOFF
INGÉNIEUR – CIVIL

— LÉGENDE —

Bâtiments		Dattiers	
Églises		Terrains Vagues	
Mosquées		Chemins de Fer	
Synagogues		Tramways	
Jardins		Tracés Projetés	

MER MEDITERRANÉE

Enregistré, exécuté et publié par l'Ing! A. NICOHOSOFF, 22, Rue Gustave Lambroso, Ramleh – ALEXANDRIE.

Bulkeley–Halte No. I [renamed Saba Pacha]: 900–950 steps, 9 minutes.

Halte No. I–Halte No. II [renamed Glymenopoulo]: 600–650 steps, 6 minutes.

Halte No. II–San Stefano: 1,200–1,300 steps, 12 and a half minutes.

San Stefano–Khediva-Mother: 1,150–1,250 steps, 12 minutes.

Alexandria–San Stefano: 10,450–11,000 steps, 1 hour 45 minutes to 2 hours.

Alexandria–Aboukir: approximately 5 hours.

Alexandria–Mex: approximately 1 and a half hours.

Aboukir–Chenndîdi: approximately 8 hours.

Geology. The alluvium offers little to geologists' observation. On the other hand, the sea coast presents interesting indications. First, the Mex rocks are striking. The clear sandstone of these rocks, mostly covered with fossil shells, stretches from Alexandria to very far west and forms most of the high Cyrenaica plateau. Ramleh and Alexandria will always have enough stones to build, even if one wanted to imitate the inimitable Cheops.

As for the age of these Neptunian lands, we find a lot of absurdities in the books on Egypt. I will correct some of them. Besides, the scholars of the French expedition under Bonaparte had already expressed their ideas. Dr. Figari Bey considers the Ramleh sandstone of the Pliocene Tertiary era. Dr. J. Jankó (Jahrbuch d. k. Ung. Geolog. Anstalt, 8., 9., 1890) in turn, takes these reefs and dunes for rocks of the Miocene Tertiary Age. What we're sure of is that there was a time when the entire coast of Ramleh, from the Libyan Desert to Aboukir, was only a series of scattered rocky islets, as Nelson Island still is nowadays, and the sea flowed freely through these islets towards the south. Today's lakes, Lake Maréotis and Lake Aboukir, were part of the sea and its shores, so their southern banks were the southern coast of the Mediterranean. According to Dr. Jankó, the Ramleh islands (the hills of today) do not belong to the Nile Delta. They are completely independent from it, having been formed by a much older tertiary layer. Dr. Jankó starts from this principle that one can only call the Nile Delta what is formed by the river and therefore comes from the Nile silt. The director Th. Fuchs more or less agrees with Dr. Jankó, but, in his opinion, the tertiary age is by no means proven. This could only be proven by distinctive fossils that have not been found until today. The Ramleh hills which consist of sandstone fall into two main groups: one is a soft, brittle and weakly cemented quartz sandstone with many debris of scale, and the other is a more consistent, fully cemented sandstone in which the quartz grains are dominant. According to Fuchs, both groups arranged in inclined layers, sometimes broken and raised, are of the quaternary era. We can observe everywhere that Ramleh, the sandy strip between the lakes (Mareotis and Aboukir) and the Mediterranean, called *Taenia alexandrina* (tapeworm) in ancient times, was formed by alluviums that had blocked the water currents' wide passages between the islands. The coast is almost entirely covered with fine sand brought by the sea (except at Aboukir). Further south, the terrain consists of sand strongly mixed with black earth, the silt deposits brought by the old Canopic branch of the Nile. Farther still, at the edge of the lakes, the pure silt of the Nile dominates. These facts fully explain the Neptunian birth of Ramleh and Alexandria.

Flora. (Phenological observations.) In the summer only a few dried out stems are seen in the desert. After the first rains in autumn, sparse greenery appears with a large quantity of various small flowers. The botanist will find two hundred interesting varieties. A very distinctive Ramleh desert plant is the "ice-plant" *(Mesembryanthemum crystallinum)*. Flora, generally quite rare, develops mostly in February and March then quickly dies. Shortly before the decay of all vegetation, the desert takes on the scarlet hue of the many red poppies

Promenade de Ramleh.

that bloom for a short time. The following plants are common in the gardens and surrounding fields: Palm trees, solitary or in groves, beautiful as nowhere else, fig trees, albizzias, casuarinas, *Schinus* (wrongly named pepper plant), gigantic sycamores, many mulberries, some almond trees, olive trees, plum trees and carob trees. Apple trees are very rare. They flower wonderfully but do not produce, or give bad little fruits, and then a few years later they perish. There are many vines and apricot trees, magnolias, bay trees and myrtles, orange trees, lemon trees, mandarin trees, tamarisks, agaves, cypress, cacti, araucarias, jacarandas (flowers of a beautiful red or blue colour), several species of ficus, Babylonian weeping willows, bamboos, oleanders, etc.

In January the almonds bloom; from January to February, apricots; January to March, violets. Lemons, oranges, mandarins, plums and apples bloom in February and March. Roses and other garden flowers bloom all year round. The beauty of the roses is extraordinary; it is for this reason that the Spanish declare in their songs that the Alexandrian rose is the most beautiful. Strawberries show their delicate flowers in January, and their delicious fruits are ripe in April. The *schinus* (wrongly named pepper tree) was transplanted from the southern hemisphere to Egypt and kept its qualities. There it flowers in the spring which is September in Egypt, and its small red berries ripen two or three months later. Cotton is sown in January and picked in the fall. Sugar cane ripens in summer and autumn, depending on the species. Wheat (or barley) is sown in November and harvested in April. Gum trees, hibiscus, begonias, daisies, poinsettias, bougainvillaea, etc. grow in the gardens. The fig tree's first leaves are in March and its fruits are in June and autumn. It loses its leaves in the last two months of the year. Albizzias (*labakh*) remain green throughout the winter. They lose their leaves in March and turn green again at the end of May. Apricot trees partially lose their leaves in

November and December. In February they bloom again and we can then see the new leaves and those that are yellowed, next to each other. Their fruits are ripe in May. Lilacs appear at Easter. The date palm blooms in spring and its fruits are ripe in October and November. They then hang below the beautiful palm leaves in large bunches of a bright garnet, with long stems. There are several species of date palms. The most remarkable are the dark ones and the yellow ones. Grapes ripen from the beginning of June to the end of August depending on the species. The Ramleh vines were very famous in the old days. Today they leave something to be desired. Mandarins are picked in November and December, and oranges in December and January. Custard apples are picked in August, September and October, and melons in spring and summer. Bananas and all vegetables are picked all year long. Bananas, dates and figs have an exquisite taste in Ramleh. Fruits, vegetables, spices, bread and oil plants have more than 150 varieties.

In all the vegetation, one can observe the influence of the weak winter of Ramleh, which resembles summer in Europe. Many plants have stopped following the temperature course and more than half of the different species of trees and bushes remain continuously green.

Fauna. Hunting and fishing are to be warmly recommended. Amateurs extend their stay to enjoy these two activities in the great outdoors. For hunting, only birds of passage cross the country during the winter in Ramleh. Starting in September, the quails, turtledoves, mermaids, orioles (our Nimrods call them "yellow") and hoopoes arrive.

The capture of quails is especially interesting. At the beginning of September, stakes of 1.5 metres to 2.5 metres are planted on the seaside. From one stake to another, high nets are stretched, sometimes over an area of 100 meters. The nets form a large pocket at their base. Quails only travel at night. They cross the sea, if the wind is favourable, and reach the shore around morning. In grazing the

Bedouin camp in Ramleh.

ground, the birds hit in force against the net and get entangled in the pocket, from which they are taken out by hand. The quails thus caught alive are exported by the thousands to Europe. By October most of them are already in Upper Egypt. They then go to Sudan where they remain until the end of January. Afterwards they return to Nubia and Upper Egypt to hatch in February. In mid-March they go to Lower Egypt towards Ramleh. In April and May, they cross the African coast to fly towards Europe.

The following birds are hunted throughout the winter: wild ducks, teals, woodcock, snipe, plovers, and Eurasian dotterels. The best hunting grounds are around the Mahmoudieh Canal, Lake Mareotis and Aboukir. Other birds stop over from December to February in Ramleh: starlings, thrushes and some blackbirds. During winter, we can still see some wagtails, robins, desert bullfinches, Swedish bluethroat *(Erithacus suecicus)*, warblers, wrens, canaries, larks, beccaficos (from August), flycatchers, horned owls, owls, sparrows (all year), nightingales (the *boulboul* all year), several species of swallows, cuckoos, carrion crows, crows, herons, sea doves, pelicans, eagles, falcons, vultures, storks, loons, etc.

The Mediterranean coast is very rich in Ramleh, especially in beautiful sea shells and marine animals. Italian, Arab and Greek fishermen go out every day with their boats and are watched from the shore with great interest. The Arabs fish with large nets, exactly as the New Testament describes it. The Europeans catch their fish by line. In the Nile there are freshwater fish which are distinguished by their ugliness. They have badly turned eyes, very ugly fins and beards. Their flesh has little taste. It is remarkable that amongst them is the electric catfish *(Malapterurus electricus)*.

Pleasures and distractions. When the night torch shines with its pale light on the landscape, the view is charming. A donkey ride in the desert towards Montazah is a pleasant excursion. There is hunting in winter and fishing all year round. The port of Alexandria is famous for boating and yacht trips. The Alexandria Boating Club, President: Jannowitz.

The warships stationed in the port, especially the English, organize regattas and sea excursions.

The Hotel and Casino San Stefano gives (mainly in summer) theatrical and artistic performances, public festivals, concerts, balls and parties. Every Thursday in summer, a military concert (English) is held. San Stefano Club.

Sporting Club between Ibrahimieh and Sidi Gaber. Great location for frequent famous races. Book club, gymkhanas. Every week there is polo, lawn tennis, golf, cricket and croquet.

In Ramleh there are over twenty lawn tennis courts. Alexandria has several societies, including the Touring Club (cyclists), Deutscher Sportverein, the British Rifle Club in Ramleh, velodrome (Roundabout), fencing company, etc.

There are theatre plays and artistic performances every day, summer and winter, in Alexandria.

Water supply. Drinking water comes from the Mahmoudieh canal, which is connected to the Rosetta branch of the Nile at Atfeh. The canal was dug in 1819 by Mohammed Ali and received its name from Mahmoud, the reigning sultan. If the water level drops, canals bring it from Cairo's surroundings. Within ten days 500,000 tons of water are poured into the canal. The pumps for Ramleh are near Abou Nawatir, from where the water reaches the reservoir located on Marelli Hill (Bulkeley). This reservoir is estimated to use 12,000^{m3} of water per day. Before use, the Nile water is filtered in large jugs of porous clay. Ibrahimieh receives water from Alexandria.

Authorities. Ramleh is a dependent of Alexandria governorate. The Governor is Sidky Pasha. The central police district for Ramleh is at

Alexandrie des bains.

Karakol Bacos. Ibrahimieh is under Moharrem Bey (Alexandria). Europeans are only under the jurisdiction of their consulates.

Consulates. In Alexandria: The French Consulate is near the Theatre Zizinia. The German Consulate is on Rue Rosette. The Austro-Hungarian Consulate is near the Theatre Zizinia. The English consulate is on Ramleh Boulevard. The Italian Consulate is on Rue de l'Eglise Copte. The Russian Consulate is on Rue Rosette. The Greek Consulate is on Rue Rosette.

Banks. In Alexandria: Anglo-Egyptian, Credit Lyonnais, Nationale and Ottoman.

Breweries. In Ramleh: Casino d'Ibrahimieh, Rosette in Ibrahimieh, Crown Brewery in Bulkeley and Casino in Khediva-Mother. In Alexandria: Dockhorn, Fink, Falk and Delacovias.

Travel offices. Cook, Gaze and Stangen in Alexandria.

Cafés. In Ramleh: Café Central, Laiterie Française; in Ibrahimieh: Café Felice; in Sidi Gaber: Café Triangle; in Bulkeley: Café International; in S. Stefano: Café Rusacci; in Abou Nawatir: Café Havakis. A cup of Frankish or Turkish coffee costs a meager piastre. They still serve lemonade, eaux-de-vies, and for smoking, the Turkish water pipe (nargileh). Cafés in Arab neighbourhoods are frequented only by the lower classes.

Clubs. In Alexandria: Cercle Khédivial and Cercle Mohamed Ali. In Ramleh: Club San Stefano, Sporting Club and the Rifle Club.

Municipal Council in Alexandria. President Chakour Bey; City Physician Dr. Gotschlich; Chief Engineer Dietrich Bey.

Schools. French schools: Rubens in Ibrahimieh, Girard in Bulkeley, Les dames de Sion (Catholic boarding school) in Fleming, Institut des Frères in Bacos, and the Parish school, Saint Elie (Greek-Orthodox) in San Stefano. A few elementary Arabic schools in Bacos. In Alexandria, there are several free and private educational establishments (French, English, German, Greek and Arabic schools) for boys and girls of all religions, and a high school managed by the Jesuits.

Churches in Ramleh. Ibrahimieh: Greek Orthodox Chapel founded by Mrs. Gogos. Sidi Gaber: Mosque. Bulkeley: English church (high-church). Fleming: Greek Catholic church, Roman Catholic chapel with Dames de Sion convent. Bacos: Catholic Church, Franciscan convent, two mosques—Chorbagi and Abou Seff. Zahrieh: Hag Radaouan Mosque. San Stefano: two Greek Orthodox churches—Saint Elie and Saint Etienne. In Alexandria: a Protestant German church, a Scottish one and several Jewish temples.

Homes. In each resort in Ramleh, there is a large number of villas for rent, winter and summer. They are rarely furnished. The price per year varies, depending on the situation and the size of the house, from 25 to 200 pounds sterling and more. The slightly higher places are preferable. (Require contract in writing.) For domestic hires, contact in Alexandria: Asile François-Joseph, Rue Tewfik. The salary varies from 35 to 60 francs per month. The author, given his relationships with Ramlites, is sometimes able to recommend villas for rent.

Hospitals. In Alexandria: Deaconesses (German and English) in Moharrem-Bey. European Hospital (French, Austrian, Italian). Greek Hospital. Government hospital (Natives).

Hotels in Ramleh. Hotel and Casino San Stefano. Management: George Nungovich Egyptian Hotels Company. Lodging 60–100, rooms for 25 piastres per day. Theatre, concerts, parties, sea baths, Club S. Stefano. Better price in winter. — Hôtel des tentes Ras el-Bar in Aboukir (Ramleh). Owner: Albert Schlesinger. Well located healing station. Tents 20 piastres and lodging 50 piastres per day. Sea bathing, hunting, fishing, sport. This hotel at Ras el-Bar is recommended for people with delicate health. — Hôtel Baghdad in San Stefano. Owner:

Le gran! Casino de l'Ibrahimieh   Alexandrie

74 Made for Pierre Agopian, Alexandria, Egypt.

Ibrahimieh. The area extending from the sea to the hills of Hadra was owned in part by Prince Ibrahim Pasha Ahmed, young son of Ibrahim Pasha, and in 1888 passed into the hands of a syndicate that gave his name to their new development.

Serpos Bey. Rooms 20 piastres and lodging 50 piastres per day. — Hôtel Beau-Rivage, Halte Laurens. Owner: Mrs. Steinschneider. Rooms 20–30 piastres and lodging 50–75 piastres per day. — Hôtel de Plaisance in Schutz. Owner: H. Mayard. 8–15 francs per day. — Hotel Miramar, Fleming. Owner: Mme. H. Buzel. 8–15 francs per day. — Pension Margherita, S. Stefano. 8–15 francs per day. — Hotels in Alexandria: Khedivial, Abbat, Canal de Suez, Continental, du Nil, d'Angleterre, Pension Ambros.

Newspapers. French: *Phare d'Alexandrie, Réforme*. English: *Egyptian Gazette*. Italian: *Messaggiere Egiziano*. Greek: *Homonoïa, Tachydromos*. Arabic: *Al-Ahram*. They all appear in Alexandria.

Bookshops. In Alexandria: Schuller, Calebotta, Bassi, de la Bourse. City library, open every day. Librarian: Nourisson.

Shops. Almost all goods and articles can be found in Alexandria, Cherif Pasha Street, Mohamed Ali Square and the vicinity. Bacos is also well stocked with small objects.

Doctors in Alexandria. Doctors: Alpar, Brandes, Burlazzi, Camerini, Ciuti, Cogniard, Colloridi, Coporcich, Démétriadis, Duca, Finzi, Goebel (surgeon), Gotschlich, Kartulis, Kornfeld, Legrand, Massa, Mauri, Morrison, Osborne (oculist), Pecnik, Roger (surgeon), Ruffer, Schiess, Semo, Torella, Valassapoulos, Valensin, Varenhorst. Dentists: Bauer, Lederer, Love, Picton, Shellard.

Doctors in Ramleh. Dr. Bérard, Colloridi, Gotschlich, Kanzki, Kartulis, Lakah, Mahmoud Hamdi, Osborne, Pecnik, Philippidis, Ruffer, Silvagni, Valensin, Zambacos.

Museum. The Graeco-Roman Museum in Alexandria is very interesting and located on Rue du Musée. It is open daily from 9 a.m. to 12 noon and 3 to 5 p.m. Curator: Dr. Comm. J. Botti.

Meteorological and hydrological observatory for Ramleh. Small private observatory. Observer: Dr. Charles Pecnik. — Observatory in Alexandria, Rue de France. The knight Pirona made his observations there for more than 26 years. Observer: J. Michaca.

Pharmacies. In Ramleh: Del Buono and Pappanicola in Schutz. Pallamaris and Galien in Bacos. Stein in Bulkeley. A drugstore in San Stefano. — In Alexandria: Ruelberg, Huber, Galetti, Lucaçi, Vaiss, Mugnier, Orphanides, Chiara and Attarine.

Posts and telegraphs. In Ramleh, each station has its post office. The central office is in Bacos. Telegraphs are in Sidi Gaber, Bacos and S. Stefano. Dispatches for Europe are sent to the English telegraph, Eastern Company, in Alexandria. The telephone is installed almost everywhere. The main Egyptian post office and a French post office are in Alexandria.

Tobacco. In each station in Ramleh there are many shops where cigarettes and tobacco are sold. For the good kind, it is preferable to go to Flick, Melachrino, Soussa, etc. in Alexandria.

Theatre. A small theatre in San Stefano gives performances on occasion. In Alexandria, the Zizinia and Monferrato theatres are only open in winter. The Alhambra (theatre and garden) and Alcazar also give performances in summer. Theatre plays: operas, operettas and comedies are always in Italian, rarely in French.

Cabs. — (1 and 2 horses.) Payment according to the price list. Tipping is not customary. Only pay at the last moment. The coachmen are never happy. They often bother travellers with requests and even threats.

Donkeys. For excursions in the surroundings, this mode being the easiest and most economical means of transport. For a trip, the price is 2 to 3 meager piasters; for an hour 3 to 5; for a morning 10 to 15 and for the whole day 20 meager piastres. A few piastres are given as tip (bakchiche).

EDITION B. SIRVEN.

ALEXANDRIA - SPORTING CLUB.

The Sporting Club.

1. Ibrahimieh.

Railway station from Ramleh, post office. Ibrahimieh is located on a long hill that stretches from the sea to Moharrem Bey and the Mahmoudieh Canal. The hill is intersected three times across its width by railways and the road from Alexandria to Ramleh. Ibrahimieh covers only a small part of the hill on the northeastern side. The highest point above sea level is 21 metres, the average height is 15 metres. The hill of Ibrahimieh is known by different names: in the east it is Ibrahimieh Hill, in the west it is Chatby Hill and in the south it is Hatt el-Nahr. The old name is Copron Hill. Between Alexandria and Ibrahimieh we see the Arab village Chatby. Arab tanneries. Towards the sea, Fort Silsileh (formerly: Lochias, Royal Palace, Royal Port, Temple of Artemis, Diabathra). Next to Chatby are the cemeteries of Alexandria. The hill of Ibrahimieh is bounded to the north by the Mediterranean, to the east by the racetrack, to the south by the Red Road and to the west by the desert.

The four cardinal points are taken approximately, since the entire coast of Ramleh runs from southwest to northeast. Before 1887, the hill was nothing but desert, part of the vast possessions of Prince Ibrahim, hence its name. The Arabs call the hill "Brhemieh," the Italians "Ibrahimieh." The engineer J. B. Maillan bought this hill in 1887 and divided the area into 500 lots.

Between the railway line and the sea to the west is Camp de César (Caesar's Camp) district and to the east the Bains de Cléopâtre (Cleopatra's Baths) district. Between the railway line and the Red Road is the Ibrahimieh district to the west and the Small Ibrahimieh to the east.

The hill consists of porous sand, so ground water flows freely. Ibrahimieh is healthy, given its elevation. The streets are usable, but leave something to be desired. Drinking water comes from Alexandria. The district police are at Moharrem Bey (Alexandria), a police station (karakol) on the Red Road.

Note: Greek Orthodox Church, founded by Gogo Nicolò di Bari. French school: Rubens. Ibrahimieh Casino. Ibrahimieh has a brewery called Crown Brewery, the first in Egypt that belongs to a Belgian company. The visit to this establishment is very interesting. The Pilsen and Bayrish beers contain little alcohol. Sea bathing: Miriantopoulo. Café Central. Bakery: Lecca. Butcher: Mursi. Building materials: Arico. Grocers: Vassili, Bartelloni, Syrica. French dairy; Café Rosette on the Red Road.

Villa Names in Ibrahimieh: Alfaropoulo, Anhoury, Beltran, Boissy, Boni, Boromeo, Buccianti, Combilis, Debono, Démétriadès, Félix, Grimaud, Hess, Kallidès, Kamel, Klonaridis, Klüppel, Maillan, Marini, Maury, Messau, Mugnier, Nahas, Ott, Pangalo, Paximadis, Perino, Prazzica, Risopoulo, Sarapata, Schopp, Scanavi, Sirdari (owners).

Hadra. Arab village near the Ramleh line. Trains stops in Hadra: Alexandria–Cairo and Alexandria–Mex. Hadra is located between the Red Road and the Mahmoudieh Canal. Near the latter passes a road from Alexandria which extends to the much praised garden of Mr. Antoniadis. Before entering Hadra, you can see Prince Ibrahim's stables on the Red Road. The large surrounding fields also belong to him.

Sporting Club. Occasional stop. Between Ibrahimieh and Sidi Gaber, a vast renowned racecourse. Polo, golf, cricket, lawn tennis and croquet, every week. Contact the Club secretary.

2. Sidi Gaber.

Post office and telegraph. Ramleh railway station. Ramleh Station for the Alexandria–Cairo express. Station for lines to Aboukir and Rosette. The Ramleh and the State railway stations are separated by the Red Road. Not far is a small Arab village.

Le Champ des Courses (Hippodrome) Alexandrie

47 Made for Pierre Agopian, Alexandria, Egypt.

The Racecourse.

Upon entering Sidi Gaber, we see Prince Ibrahim's villa on the Red Road. Next to it, there is a road leading to the Mahmoudieh Canal and the Antoniadis Garden. The palaces and harems of wealthy Egyptian dignitaries and pashas are located on the Mahmoudieh Canal. These are their summer residences.

On the sea side, there are several buildings, formerly the summer residence of Khedive Ismail (1863–1879). Today they are transformed into English barracks, called "Camp Moustapha".

Halte Moustapha Pacha. Stop of the new line: Alexandria–Khediva-Mother. Since 1893 there has always been an English battalion here. The soldiers are housed in twelve wooden barracks, four villas are for officers, and there are Soldiers' Institute, Officers' Mess, as well as canteens. There is an exercise field. One of the four palaces is uninhabited. The non-commissioned officers have theirs, the canteens and the battalion offices occupy the other two. To the southeast there is a tall tower, the old reservoir.

Note: Café Felice. Police station.

Villa Names in Sidi Gaber: Bodenstein, Brès, Bret, Buhagiar, Cintillaki, Khalil, P. P. Jésuites of Alexandria, Lucaçi, Marzuki, Peel, Smith, Swoboda, Vinga.

Hagar el-Nawatieh. From Sidi-Gaber, the railway line from Alexandria to Cairo goes southeast and crosses, on a swing bridge, the Mahmoudieh Canal. The part located on the southwestern side of this railway line is known as Hagar el-Nawatieh. There are groves of palm and fig trees and then plowed land. The arable land runs alongside a small saltwater lake, named Lake Hadra or Mallaha. Its edges are covered with thick brushwood. It is the meeting point of the nimrods.

Lake Hadra is an offshoot of Lake Marioût. It is separated from it by the dikes of the Mahmoudieh Canal. Lake Marioût is 2.5 metres below sea level. Its surface area is 40,000 hectares. In antiquity, it was connected to the Nile by several canals and served as a port for the residents of Alexandria. The shores were famous then for their fertility. The abundant vines produced an excellent white wine which was exported in clay jugs to all the Roman Empire, as the nectar of every feast. When the French expedition under Bonaparte arrived, the lake was almost dry. In April 1801, the English, to separate the French garrison in Alexandria from the mainland, let sea water flow into the old lake bed. Many drowned and several villages disappeared in the flood. On the coast, duck hunting is pleasant. Salt and potash are extracted there (Egyptian Salt Co.).

Abou Nawatir. East of the Cairo Railway. Western slope of Marelli Hill. Plantations of palm and fig trees. An Arab village on the bank of the Mahmoudieh Canal. Many (three-masted) sailing boats transporting goods in the canal are obliged to wait at the swing bridge for trains to pass. Pumps carry water to the reservoir. The best way to reach Abou Nawatir is through the Bacos and Zahrieh roads. There begins a grove of palm trees several kilometres long to the east.

One and a half kilometres from the village, on the seaside close to the Red Road, there is a colony of villas of the same name. Next to it: the Halte Moustapha Pacha and the Camp.

Note: Café Havakis.

Villa names: Adem, Bossone, Callendar, Faik, Farag, Farghali, Havakis, Kamat, Khayat, Lazaris, Maurel, Picton, Sabek, Soliman.

3. Bulkeley.

Bulkeley (pronounced: Bálkli). Mr. Bulkeley was one of the founders of the Ramleh Railway. Station. Post office. The Ramleh Railway junction, the old line passes through Fleming, Bacos, Schutz and ends at San Stefano. The new line heads towards the sea by Halte No. 1 and Halte No. 2 at the Khediva-Mother Palace. Bulkeley is located between two

142 ALEXANDRIA. — *Train from Ramleh, station at Sidi-Gaber* . — LL.

Sidi Gaber Station.

hills: the hill of Moss, near the sea and the hill of Marelli. Most of the villas are built in the valley and on both sides. People visiting Ramleh should not miss going to Marelli Hill to enjoy the magnificent view, most easily reached by passing in front of the Marelli and Marshall villas. View: To the west Alexandria, the lighthouse, Lake Mareotis and beyond, the elevations of the Libyan desert. To the north: the Mediterranean. To the east: lovely view of Ramleh. It feels like a city on the Italian coast. Further, palm groves and the rugged desert towards Montazah and Aboukir. To the south: the Mahmoudieh Canal, Lake Mareotis, plowed land and then immense groves of palm trees.

Note: English church (high-church). — Girard private French school. — Stein pharmacy. — Crown Brewery. — Café Triangle. — Grocery: Kyriacou, Vafea. — Sea bathing cabins: Stanley Bay. — A very nice public garden called Aldersoneum, founded by Mr. Geo. Alderson.

Villa Names in Bulkeley: Adrien, Alderson, Allen, Amin, Baruch, Calliga, Carver, Celi, Crafton, Cumbo, Duport, Felonico, Fischer, Haselden, Hicks, Karam, Kerati, Lifonti, Lindi, Luzzatto, Marelli, Marshall, Maurino, Meimarachi, Monferrato, Morice, Mors, Moss, Peake, Royle, Ruffer, Sagrestani, Seeger, Simond, Stross, Valensin, Xuereff, Zambacos (owners).

4. Fleming.

Railway station, post office. Fleming is named after one of the founders of the Ramleh Railway. Numerous villas, close to one another, stretch from Bulkeley to San Stefano, but one can still see large empty lands. All the villas adjoin with no possible continuity. The division into stations is difficult and has no value other than orientation.

Note: Greek Catholic Chapel. — Hotel Miramar. — Les Dames de Sion (Catholic boarding school). — Police station. — Grocery stores: Pantasis, Mitzos and Scutaris. — Bakery Zetopoulo.

Villa Names in Fleming: Anhoury, Birch, Busic (Fleur de Lis), Caillard, Caprara, Carver, Cattaui, Chiscas, Dumreicher, Falanga, Gabriel, Haïcalis, Haselden, Hewat, Hoyami, Kalliadès, Karam, Lakah, Lanner, Mourès, Neroutzos, Ninci, Orel, Polzi, Rothacker, Royle (Ernani), Soussa, Suarès, Sursock, Takla, Terni, Williams, Wilson, Zogheb.

Halte No. 1. [renamed Saba Pasha] Station of the Bulkeley–San Stefano–Khediva-Mother Palace line. Near the Falanga villa. In the north-east, on the seaside, rises the Dumreicher Hill on which a villa of the same name is built. The coast here is quite bizarre.

5. Bacos.

Railway station, telegraph, Ramleh central post office and police center. The Karakol is in the Rue du Bazar. Bacos is Ramleh's central point. Its district of European villas extends to a heavily populated Arab bazaar. The bazaar is a lively long street with some narrow alleys where any possible article is sold in a large number of small Arab and Greek shops.

Note: Catholic Church. — Franciscan Convent. — Two mosques. — Institut des Frères with day school and boarding school (French). — Some elementary schools in the Arab quarter. — Pharmacies: Pallamaris, Galien. — Café Central, Bar Cumidi. Economides (bakery), Mifsoud (butcher), Grocery stores: Pafiti, Zammit, Andrea, Joseph, Spreafico, Atfendouli, Cumidi.

Villa Names in Bacos: Abou-Souoûd, Anagnostaki, Bacos Halil, Bacos V., Bavastro, Boccia, Camilleri, Cattani, Chahin, Chersich, Chini, Chorbagi, Diacono, Fakak, Garofalo, Girard, Glymenopoulo, Hamid, Hicks, Kalliadès, Joannou, Lombardo, Mercinier, Morgos, Rassim, Riaz, Silvagni, Spanopoulo, el-Tourki, Toussoun, Zervudachi.

Halte No. 2. [renamed Glymenopoulo] Located towards the sea. Bulkeley–Khediva-Mother line. Next to the Glymenopoulo villa. At the

ALEXANDRIE.-MOSQUÉE DE SIDI-GOBER

Sidi Gaber Mosque.

shore: Coast Guard barracks, some sea bathing cabins.

Zahrieh. Arab village located southwest of Bacos, at the interior of the country. Railway station for Alexandria–Aboukir and Alexandria–Rosette. A road from Bacos leads through Zahrieh to Abou Nawatir and to the Mahmoudieh Canal. Here a grove of palm trees begins. Near the road, there is an Arab cemetery. The walk in Zahrieh is interesting.

Souk. South of Bacos. Railway station (see Zahrieh). Souk is behind the bazaars of Bacos.

Gabrial. Southeast of Bacos. Railway station (see Zahrieh). Gabrial is located in the extension of the bazaar road in Bacos. Crossing the railway line at Gabrial, we get to the fields and admire the groves of palm trees. In the northeast is the desert with a slight hill formation. The road passes in front of the Diamanti brickyard towards Mandara. A bit further are the Blue House and the Pink House. Nice walk.

6. Seffer.

Railway station. Post office. All stations, starting from Bulkeley, were named after the founders of Ramleh Railway.

Villa Names in Seffer: Andrès, Boghos-Nubar, Cherubini, Crouzier, Ghelal, Ibrahim-Halim, Jones, Mohsen, Müller, Nicolaïdès, Seff A., Seff H., Sinadino, Suarès, Tachau.

7. Schutz.

Ramleh railway station. Post office. Most villas are built to the east.

Note: Hôtel de Plaisance. — Pharmacies: Del Buono and Pappanicola. — Bakeries: Chiron and Guillo. — Grocery stores: Athanasi, Kamizani, Kyriaco, Petmezaki, Romano, Stamati. —American Mission.

Villa Names in Schutz: Adib, Athanassiadis, Azmy, Bally, Bollas, Camilleri, Caridis, Cristodoulou, Despinas, Dikéos, Dimitriou, Fabbri, Farès, Garofalo, Haicalis, Hanem, Livadà, Maestracci, Magnin, Mavropoulo, Metaxopo, Milanopoulo, Portocaloglu, Sirgunelli, Skormann, Stabile, Tambacopoulo, Tonna, Varouti, Wilme, Zancarol.

Ramleh Station of the Alexandria–Aboukir and Alexandria–Rosette lines. From Schutz, we get to Ramleh from the east. Ramleh is in the middle of the desert. Its charming surroundings are very inviting for walks. To the south, there is an Arab village and groves of palm trees. Outside is the Villa Metaxopoulo.

8. San Stefano.

Ramleh railway station. Post and telegraph office. To the west are the Zizinia Hill and the villa of the same name. In front of San Stefano, the Red Road divides: two junctions cross the new railway line and lead to the Hotel and Casino San Stefano, a third crosses the old line and heads east, then north and finally ends near the sea at Khediva-Mother Palace.

Note: Hotel and Casino San Stefano. Theater, concerts, balls. Two large sea bathing establishments. Club San Stefano. — Hotel Baghdad, owner: Serpos Bey. — Pension Margherita. — Two Greek churches: St. Elie and San Stefano. — School of the Greek church: St. Elie. — Drugstore. — Café International and Café Rusacci, both on the Red Road. — De Biasi, gardener; Stefanos, grocer.

Villa Names in San Stefano: Adib, Andelaft, Antoniadis, Arcondoulis, Aslan, Asprea, Avierino, Benachi, Chasseaud, Chiozza, Comstantinidis, Dalil, Dimitriou, Gianacli, Haïdemenos, Horn, Huri, Kindineco, Lagoudakis, Limpritis, Mazloum, Melachrino, Pangalo, Raïssis, Ralli, Skouffos, Statopoulo, Steinschneider, Trekaki, Tsoumakos, Zervudachi, Zizinia, Zuro.

Halte Zizinia. A Bulkeley line stop at the Khediva-Mother Palace at Zizinia Hill.

Moustapha Pasha Barracks. Originally the palace of Prince Moustapha Fazil Pasha, brother of Khedive Ismail and his heir apparent until primogeniture was established, it became a British army garrison.

Halte Laurens. Between San Stefano and the Khediva-Mother Palace.

9. Khediva-Mother Palace.

Ramleh railway station. Post Office. Railway line: Bulkeley–San Stefano–Khediva-Mother.

At the station, close to the sea, is the Palace (summer residence) of the Khediva-Mother, surrounded by beautiful parks. The railway crosses a hill. It is interesting to examine the path that was cut in the rock. It descends in a large curve to the south to connect Ramleh station to the line from Alexandria to Aboukir. This route is not in circulation. To the southeast is the Arab village of Siouf (name meaning "daggers"). Nearby is a grove of palm trees, probably the most beautiful in the vicinity of Ramleh. In the middle of the desert, the palm trees seem more graceful, ethereal. The grove is cut in the centre by the dike of the Aboukir railway line. South of this line is a group of houses called Dar-Bâla. Towards the east there are several Arab houses built on hills and two picturesque windmills. Climb to the east of the palm grove on one of the hills and you will see the desert's delightful landscape: a huge stretch of sand interrupted, here and there, by a few hills. Towards the sea is a mosque with its slender minaret. This mosque is known as Sidi Bishr. The group of houses located between the Siouf village and Sidi Bishr is called Babên. Behind it is the Dar-Isi village. The attempts to plant in the middle of the desert are very curious. The border of this nursery is lined with fig trees, vines and small palm trees and on top, as sand and windbreaks, is a hedge of dry palm branches.

Villa Names at the Khediva-Mother Palace: Assad, Cristou, Fenderl, Idris-Ragheb, Laurens, Archduke Louis Salvator of Austria (3 villas, very beautiful garden), Menasce, Pietrettini, Stavraki, Stevenson, Vacher. The center of the villas is at Halte Laurens. — Hôtel Beau Rivage at Halte Laurens. Owner: Mrs. Steinschneider. — Casino (Café and brasserie) at Khediva-Mother.

10. House of the Devil.

In Arabic: *Bayt el-Afrit*. This name is given by the Arabs to a small villa that a misanthrope built in the old days in the middle of the desert. People recount all kinds of terrible actions and fabulous stories that the reader will exempt me from repeating. It takes twenty to thirty minutes on a donkey to get there from San Stefano along the sea in the eastern direction. Around the House of the Devil is barren desert. By the sea there is a promontory (Butterfly Cape). In the rock is an artificial cavity, called Hole of the Devil or Bir Massoud where the waves break with force. Next to it is a beautiful little rocky bay. There are a few tiny islets, amongst them the islet Ghezireh. From the Khediva-Mother Palace to Mandara, the landscape is bare desert like the Sahara. Poor Bedouin tents, here and there, complete the illusion.

Through this desert, Bonaparte entered Alexandria after having disembarked at Aboukir and crossed Ramleh. One will find descriptions of Bonaparte's historiographers exaggerated when speaking of the difficulties of walking through this desert.

11. Mandara.

Small Arab village. Railway station to Aboukir. Post office. The distance between the two stations Ramleh (Schutz) and Mandara is of one hour fifteen minutes to one and a half hours on foot, but the path through the sand is tiring and it is faster to go by donkey. The trip gives a characteristic idea of the desert. As far as the eye can see, nothing but sand, some bare peaks and considerable moving sand dunes. The appearance changes in Mandara with a thin vegetation of moors.

Note: Villa Goadar.

Bulkely Station named after Captain Bulkeley, a board member of the Ramleh Railway Company.

12. Montazah.

Summer residence of the Viceroy of Egypt. Aboukir railway station (private station of His Highness the Khedive). Post and telegraph office. The distance from Mandara to Montazah is about twelve minutes on foot. Montazah is the idol of S.A. the Khedive. This magical creation, this princely bijou on the edge of the Eleusinian Sea, excites all those who pass by and honours the exquisite taste and knowledge of its royal author.

Note: Huge desert park, surrounded by a hedge. Two palaces on the highest hills. Many private villas of the viceroy. Small mosque. At the coast, interesting formation of reefs (ice of Idothea).

19. 6. 08.

N. 156 - *Alexandrie - Station de Bacos*

Bacos Station. The area was once owned by the Bacos family, later broken up into individual lots and sold off for housing and commercial use. Postcard dated 1908.

144 - ALEXANDRIA - SIDI-BISH BEACH

"The three tiers of cabins were arranged along our favorite cove in a huge semi-circle rather like a theater. From there, we had a view facing King Farouk's palace in the distance... Most of the people who frequented this beach — Syrians and wealthy Egyptians — would usually sit fully dressed in the front covered part of their cabins, eating pistachios and watching the deep blue sea." —Esther Zimmerli Hardman, *From Camp Caesar to Cleopatra's Pool.*

No. 186 **ALEXANDRIΣ** — Plage Glymenopoulo

Edit. S. N. Grivas
Photo Ververis

"Everyone knew each other on Glymenopoulo Beach, which the Syrians colonised in the same way that the Jews monopolized Stanley Beach near by. They felt at home and among their own kind – so much so that they would express loud surprises if a Coptic or Muslim family had the bad form to plant its sun umbrella there." —Robert Solé, *Birds of Passage.*

Stanley Bay circa 1890.

"Stanley Bay was distinctly down-market—a huge semicircle of beach huts giving onto concrete promenades—crowded, cosmopolitan, and lively, with itinerant peanut sellers and gully-gully men, who did conjuring tricks with live baby chickens." —Penelope Lively, *Oleander, Jacaranda*.

Hotel and Casino San Stefano

Samir Raafat

In his recollections of Ramleh, Dr. Charles Pecnik remarked that Hotel Casino San Stefano was managed by the Egyptian Hotels Company owned by hospitality czar George Nungovich Bey.

"Any one of the hotel's 100 rooms could be rented for 25 piasters per day with a favourable discount in winter. Amenities included a theatre, a concert hall and a private beach, certainly more than that which is offered by the nigh yet more expensive Baghdad Hotel belonging to Serpos Bey."

When Pecnik wrote these words in 1901, the fin de siècle hotel was in its fourteenth year. Constructed in 1886–87, the original Hotel San Stefano (it changed ownership and appearances several times) was conceived by Boghos Nubar Pasha, son of Armenian statesman and sometime Prime Minister of Egypt Nubar Nubarian. A graduate of the Ecole Central in Paris, Boghos was infatuated with the casinos and seaside resorts dotting the Franco-Belgian coast between the fashionable towns of Deauville and Ostende. The result was Ramleh-Les-Bains' Casino San Stefano.

Renaissance architecture and belle époque ambiance notwithstanding, other European ingredients also made it across the Mediterranean.

On 24 May 1906, the Casino's menu featured a range of continental dishes. Sample this:

Baron d'agneau Renaissance
Medaillons de foie gras à la gelée
Petit poids nouveaux à l'anglaise
Aiguilletes de dindonneaux
Rôtis à la broche
Salade de saison
Bombe marquise
Friandises
Dessert

No wonder San Stefano was so highly recommended by His Imperial Highness Archduke Louis Salvator of Habsburg, an Alexandria regular. Another royal gourmet was Egypt's Austrian-educated khedive. Whenever he stayed at his mother's neighbouring hilltop *saray* (later nicknamed Palace of Sorrows), Abbas Helmi II would pop in for Viennese pastries, a welcome diversion when he was not supervising the construction of his seaside palais de chasse, Montazah Palace.

In Pecnik's days San Stefano was reached by horse carriage via Strada Rossa or Red Street (afterwards King Fouad Avenue now Tariq el-Horeya), so named because it was covered with reddish potsherds from the ruins of Roman Alexandria. The Corniche would be introduced much later. Alternately, there was the legendary Alexandria tramway which, in 1890, peaked at twenty-four trains per day. Both the Bacos and Schutz tram lines ended at the San Stefano terminus. A line was extended eastwards in 1909 in time for the inauguration of Victoria College, a school which subsequently made Middle East history, its fate crossing that of the casino-hotel.

Had Pecnik counted the chairs belonging to the seaside casino-hotel he would have found that 5,000 chaise longues were barely sufficient on Sundays. Moreover, the waiting list to join the genteel San Stefano Club was twice as long as its 425 membership. As the Eleusian Riviera—a term used by Pecnik to describe Ramleh—became increasingly accessible, the casino-hotel owners decided to act in response to these welcome statistics so that Nicolas Sabagh, the Syrian manager, commissioned architect Leon Stienon of the Alexandria Municipality (and part-time Dutch Consul-General) to add a new a western wing. In those days, the much-enlarged hotel was run by

The district is named after Count Stefanos Zizinias who had received it as a gift from Mohamed Ali Pasha for services rendered. He built a church, probably a private chapel, which he named San Stefano.

Alexandria's maverick hotelier, signor Luigi Steinschneider who later became the director of Zamalek's Gezira Palace Hotel (now Marriott). Both hotels were then owned by Les Grands Hotels d'Egypte ex Nungovich Hotels.

But what about the Baghdad Hotel Pecnik referred to? Well, it appears Hotel Baghdad stood a stone's throw from Casino San Stefano thus its main competitor in the Ramleh area. It was managed by Madame W. de Belinsky et Garanilsh who, like George Nungovich, also hailed from Central Europe. For austerity reasons brought on by World War I, both establishments merged becoming the San Stefano Palace Hotel and Casino which was now fully owned by Les Grands Hotels d'Egypte S.A. ex Nungovich Hotels.

The leading shareholder and director general of the Grands Hotels d'Egypte was Egypt's undisputed hospitality baron the Swiss Charles Baehler. During the interwar period he was responsible for running Egypt's top hotels and casinos from Alexandria to Aswan all of which, and up until World War II, were either directly owned or managed by the above company as well as by The Egyptian Hotels Limited also presided by Baehler.

Like what happened during World War I, the following World War also had devastating effects on Egypt's hospitality industry. One of the many collateral damages was Hotel and Casino San Stefano.

When he returned from England on 10 October 1939, in time for the new school year, Mr. Walter Ralph Reed, the apocryphal headmaster of Victoria College, learned he was henceforth the quasi director of the San Stefano casino-hotel. At the outbreak of WWII, the British army had transformed his school into a makeshift military and navy hospital. In return, the empty Hotel and Casino San Stefano was "borrowed" from its new owner, Mr. Albert Metzger (owner of the Cecil Hotel), and transformed into a Victoria College in extremis.

If the new premises were not the perfect substitute, bewildered students soon discovered how a grand ballroom could make an excellent skating rink. Likewise, schoolmasters were more than satisfied with their appointed suites.

Casino San Stefano.

Khedivial Palace, Ramleh, built in 1888 by order of Khedive Tewfik Pasha. Postcard dated 1905.

N. 133 - *Alexandrie* - *Villa de S. A. la Khédiva-Mère, à San-Stéfano*

Villa of the Khediva-Mother, also known as Saray el-Hazina (Palace of Sorrows or Palace of the Sad One) where the mother of Khedive Abbas Helmi II mourned her husband, Khedive Tewfik.

On Montazah Palace

A. B. de Guerville
New Egypt, 1906

I had something to say in regard to the railway at present being laid down, at Abbas Helmi's private expense, between Alexandria and Tripoli. Knowing my interest in these questions, his Highness expressed the desire that, before my departure from Egypt, I should pass the day with him in making a short tour of inspection of the new line. On this occasion it was at the Palace of Montazah that I was received by the Khedive, shortly before 9 a.m. Of all the Khedivial Palaces Montazah is the least known. In fact, with the exception of his intimate friends, a few advisers and others invited there for special purposes, no one knows Montazah: it is considered as a sanctuary, where the public is not admitted, and where official functions are generally taboo. What is vaguely known of it is that, only a few years ago, the ground covered by this property was a wilderness of sand dunes, which Abbas Helmi, with his customary energy, has transformed into a garden of delight. My train took me to the private station at Montazah, where I found a carriage waiting.

The entrance to the estate is guarded by immense gates of stone, in the semblance of a citadel; behind the beautiful avenues of trees, lined with flower-beds and nurseries, at the end of which, and in the midst of clumps of trees, two white Palaces overlook the sea, whose blue stretches far into the distance to mix with the deeper azure of the sky, whilst between the two gleam the white and graceful sails of many native craft. On the immense terrace of the Palace his Highness awaited me and led me into his study, a large room, bright and sunny. Here everything speaks of the works which interest the Sovereign. The walls are covered with maps and plans of his estates, the tables loaded with reports and estimates. Behind his desk I noticed a large photograph of a powerful locomotive, "belonging," his Highness explained, "to the Northern Railway Company of France, and on which, between Paris and Calais, I once did seventy-eight miles an hour." A few minutes later we were seated in a small trap drawn by two very old ponies.

"These are the first I ever had," said the Khedive, "given to me as a child to teach me to drive. Would you believe it that they are twenty-five years old? They live here happy and peaceful in quiet retirement. I only use them now for short drives, but you will see what pluck they still have and how they rush their hills."

Following a beautiful road, planted with trees, we reached a quay of dressed stone, which runs round the entire bay of Montazah, and forms an excellent harbour.

"Here," said the Khedive, "I have wished to have a home for spring and autumn. I began modestly, buying a few acres of sand dunes. To them I brought the water of the Nile, and immediately, the sand, transformed into soil, became fruitful, trees and flowers sprang up. Then, little by little, I added and added, until now I have created quite an estate, consisting today of 4000 feddans.

"First of all I built a small Palace for my own use; later I had a second Palace built for my family in a veritable oasis. The children are so happy here and enjoy their perfect liberty so much that it is a pleasure to bring them."

Round about the Palace, scattered in the grounds, are summer-houses, grottos, masses of flowers, wild and cultivated, and in a little creek, shallow and sheltered, the salt-water bath for the young Princes. Further on are large hen-houses and rabbit hutches, the latter on a rocky piece of soil where the rabbits cannot burrow and escape;

Montazah Palace.

a monster dovecot, containing thousands of birds, from the top of which can be had a superb view of the estate and the Mediterranean coast line as far as Alexandria. Across the fields, ablaze with poppies, the road leads past fir plantations to a small park where fifteen thousand mulberry bushes have been planted, the leaves of which serve for food for innumerable silkworms. Thence we passed to the farms, the stables, and, lastly, to the engine-house, where two enormous dynamos furnish the electric light necessary.

"I will show you," said his Highness, "the use to which we put this power in the daytime. Come in here and have a look at the joiners' shop and the saw-mill. Here we make the doors, windows, all the woodwork required by all the houses on all my estates, as well as the finer class of work, such as the Arabic carving for my Palaces."

It was a pleasant sight, this up-to-date carpenters' shop, with its workmen smiling and happy, stopping their work to greet us. His Highness had a word for all, examining their work, praising, criticising. Many of the workmen had been in his service for more than ten years. With his workmen as with his servants, if they do their work well, the Khedive is an excellent master. He does for them all that he can, but he is exacting and expects everything in return. The workmen were well-dressed, and I noticed with astonishment that one of them was indulging in beautiful socks and patent leather pumps. "Don't be surprised," said the Khedive; "he comes from Alexandria, and the Alexandrians are the most coquettish people in the world. They would rather starve than be ill-dressed." And I, astonished at the elegance of the fair ladies I had seen there!

We stopped for a moment before a small building containing the private telegraph and telephone of his Highness. The Khedive has found means to be independent of the English in this matter, and is able to wire to any place in Europe without making use of the English cables. This has been accomplished by the simple expedient of uniting Montazah by a private wire with the Ottoman telegraphs, which run from the frontier to Constantinople by way of Asia Minor. Montazah being connected by telephone with the other Khedivial Palaces, his Highness is thus quite independent.

Through an avenue bordered with orange-trees in flower, and lined with nurseries of young apricot and peach-trees, we returned to the Palace for lunch. In the large dining-room, the enormous table was bare, but at a small table in a bow window two places were laid. The lunch was excellent, and during its course I had occasion to admire the exquisite service of gold, which I was glad to hear had come from Paris, from Leroy in fact. It was during this lunch that I had the opportunity of discussing the question of religion with his Highness. I was aware that the Khedive was very religious, and that on this question his intransigeance was extreme. Whilst respecting the other religions which are established in Egypt, he absolutely forbids any foreign interference in the affairs of the religion of which in Egypt he is head. The English are well aware of this fact, and have clearly declared that they have no desire to interfere.

"It is a question," he said to me, "on which I consult my conscience alone, and nothing can influence it. They could cut my head off before I should renounce one of these rights or duties which I consider sacred. In this question I have my whole people with me, and they, no more than I, would permit the smallest attack on our beliefs."

"I have heard it asserted, Sir, in certain quarters, that you had a dream of replacing, with the help of England, the Sultan as the head of the Mussulman world, of seizing Mecca, and being proclaimed Chief of Islam."

"That is nonsense," replied his Highness, shrugging his shoulders, "a slander put into circulation by men to whose interest it is to harm me in the eyes of the Sultan."

The tower of Montazah Palace.

"Then, Sir, to put it in a different way, do you not believe that England may have thought of making use of your Highness and of the Mussulmans of Egypt and India to counteract German influence at Constantinople?"

"Thoughts come and thoughts go. Englishmen may have had such ideas, but I doubt it. They should know by this time that I would not lend myself to any combination which would have the effect of allowing a Christian nation to influence the destinies of Islam. And besides," he added, "I fail to see in what way England would benefit."

My own opinion is that it would be no advantage to England to increase the power of the Khedive and to put into his hands, with the hope of controlling it, the immense power of Islam, which would enable him one day to rise, if he wished, against his protectors with a very real chance of success—for we know what Mussulman fanaticism can do once it is roused.

Immediately after lunch we left the Palace for the station, where we found the train of which his Highness makes use on his excursions along the Mariout line. It was composed of a locomotive, almost entirely covered with brass, brilliantly polished, whilst the latter part was formed by a glass-panelled salon, from whence the Sovereign himself could drive the train. To this unique engine was attached a large saloon car and an ordinary carriage for the servants, who had brought with them our five o'clock tea, or rather ices.

Rapidly covering the distance between Montazah and Alexandria with its suburbs, we arrived at the terminus of the State Railways, the station and sheds of which serve equally for his Highness's line. On all sides lay enormous heaps of rails, bolts, and nuts, for use on the new line. At a short distance from the station, the railway crosses, by an embankment some three miles in extent, the Lake of Mariout, composed, as one could tell from the enormous blocks of salt alongside the embankment, of salt water. The new line has now a length of sixty miles, not, as many suppose, across barren desert, but through highly cultivated land, a large quantity of which his Highness has bought.

Grand receiving hall of Montazah Palace.

Montazah Palace

Samir Raafat

According to court chronicler Ahmed Shafik Pasha, the location of the late nineteenth-century Montazah Palace came about during a moonlight trip by Khedive Abbas Helmi. At the time, Alexandria's eastern border was demarcated by his mother's Palace of Sorrows (a.k.a. Saray el-Ramleh), at what later became known as Victoria tram terminal. Beyond this point it was all sandy hills, beaches and bays pockmarked with palm trees.

"With him on this particular moonlight escapade was his secretary Rolier Bey, Ali Shaheen Bey from Protocol and myself, along with a forty-person retinue including a musical band," says Shafik. All participants rode "Makaria" donkeys. The first stop was at Sidi Bishr where a sheikh by the same name is buried. "As we continued eastwards we ran into what must have been an old fortification from the Mohammed Ali days with a few rusty cannons still in evidence."

Fascinated by the topography which included several grottos, various hilltops and a speck of an island, Khedive Abbas decided to build a summer palace in these parts. Enquiring as to who owned the surrounding land, he was told that except for a small plot of land on which stood a wooden hut belonging to the wealthy Alexandrian Monsieur Augustino Sinadinos, the entire land belonged to the Coast Guard Department, which accounted for the two remaining lookout points and a few old cannons from the days of Viceroy Mohammed Ali.

Hereafter was born the salamlik designed by incumbent court engineer Fabricius Bey with a few changes subsequently introduced by the khedive's favourite architect, the Austrian Antonio Lasciac. As for the landscaping, flora and fauna (including gazelles), this was left entirely to Abbas Helmi's whim. Eagerly assisting him in these mundane tasks was his Hungarian paramour, Countess May von Torok, whom he eventually married (and later divorced).

According to Shafik, the name "Montazah" was chosen by courtier Mahmoud Shukry Pasha, head of the government's Turkish Diwan.

The world-famous haremlik was added during the reign of King Fouad [designed by court architect E. Verrucci Bey between 1923 and 1928]. It would later become a cultural landmark as an international casino during the short-lived administration of the Italian-run Montazah-Mokattam Company, which had leased Montazah Palace shortly after the 1952 coup that toppled the monarchy.

Foyer and great hall of Montazah Palace.

Nouzha Gardens

The public garden is to be found alongside the Mahmoudieh Canal, a little beyond Palace No. 3, the summer residence in Alexandria of the Crown Prince, where court balls are given. Every Friday and Sunday the roads that lead to the Garden are virtually crisscrossed with elegant vehicles driving up and down, showing off the magnificence of the great city. The garden is a huge park with shady paths, varied planting, landscaped areas, in the centre of which sits an elegant bandstand, where on Friday and Sunday afternoons military bands play concerts of European and Arab music.

E. François-Levernay, *Directory of Egypt for the year 1872–1873.*

The most exotic plants are to be admired in hothouses, giant ferns from Australia, arborescent ferns from Java, rare camelias and strange orchids. However, I prefer those long pathways bordered by dreamy palm trees, somewhat melancholy with their feathery palm leaves, solitary pathways, so far from the urban crowd and so favourable to escape, which call up visions of Samarkand. I love that rose garden where all varieties of roses flourish: delicate toy roses, the French roses in the fullness of their noble bloom, yellow and golden tea roses, red and white velvety roses, a delight for the eyes. I also love the orange groves, when the ground is strewn with tiny corollas of white wax, where you are almost intoxicated by the sweet, captivating fragrance which is so intense that those passing down the road, near the canal, lift up their heads, dilate their nostrils and dream of paradise.

In the Antoniadis Garden there are no flowerbeds constantly being renewed as in Nouzha, but I love its century-old trees and its most deserted-looking corners. I never fail to turn towards the statue of Venus looking at herself in her mirror, and the idea of a descendant of Ulysses gathering together the statues of Neptune, Christopher Columbus, Juno and Amerigo Vespucci in one alley of his adopted country always makes me smile.

Fernand Leprette, "Alexandria, Gate of the West" in *Egypt Land of the Nile.*

Alexandria – Antoniadis Gardens

The palace and garden of Sir John Antoniadis (1818–1895), an Alexandrian Greek with French citizenship, president of the Alexandria Greek community, Consul-General of Belgium, knighted by Queen Victoria. Built as a miniature version of Versailles in the late 1850s or early 1860s on the Mahmoudieh Canal, then home to the palatial residences of Alexandrian society, the estate was donated by Sir John's son, Anthony, to the Alexandria Municipality in 1918.

ALEXANDRIE - Au Jardin Nouzha.

Nouzha Gardens.

ALEXANDRIE. Jardin Nouzha.

Nouzha Gardens.

The Mahmoudieh Canal

Mohamed Ali Pasha thought of digging a navigable canal to ship crops from Egypt's upper, middle and lower provinces to Alexandria without passing through the Rosetta strait on the Nile estuary with its difficult, dangerous passage and frequent drownings. He assembled all seven Lower Egypt governors who agreed to assign Shaker Effendi, the Turkish engineer, to draft and execute the work, and that its entrance should be in el-Atf village below the city of Fouah, with a width of 30 metres, an average depth of 3.65 metres, and length of some 80,000 metres. Every governor would deploy workers and baskets in proportion to the population of his governorate, distributed as follows: Giza 30,000; Beheira 50,000; Qalyoubia 30,000; Menoufia 120,000; Sharqia 25,000; Mansoura 15,000; and Gharbia 130,000; with a total of 400,000 men.

The governors camped at the head of their governorates. There was a tent for each village. Their diet was onions, beans, carrots and corn bread. Each village was responsible for excavating a part of the canal based on the size of its population. When its work was done, it was discharged and returned home.

The Turkish engineer who drafted the canal instead of drawing it as a straight line, drew a crooked line without respecting the requirements or performing a topographical survey due to his ignorance of geodesy.

The works started in 1818 by digging 3.65 metres with a width of 30 metres. This resulted in changing levels of the canal bed at different points. When digging reached the dam between Aboukir and Mareotis lakes, work came to a halt. Bewildered, they didn't know how to bypass this passage. They dismissed the workers, who returned to their governorates.

At that point, the Pasha summoned me to Alexandria in March 1819, and instructed me to finish the canal and cautioned me not to change the existing drawing which had become a fact. I accepted his assignment and brought the Egyptian students I had trained to assist me and supervise my works.

I started with two operations to level the land, one from Alexandria to el-Atf and the Nile, and the second from the Nile to Alexandria. I got a slight difference from which I took an average to determine the depth of the canal bed and planted wooden pegs 365 metres apart along the canal upon which I indicated the depth required. After these arrangements, fellahin arrived from different governorates with hoes and baskets, led by the governors' headmen, correcting the measure of the canal's depth and banks, with my students lined up next to the pegs marked with the depth.

I also rectified some curves that did not meet requirements. I supervised the work daily on horseback back and forth between Alexandria and el-Atf. In parallel, I worked on bridges to contain the canal within the path between Aboukir and Mariout lakes along 2,500 meters by building strong walls and lime brackets on supports in the water. All these works were completed in December 1820. Inauguration of the water flow connecting the Nile and Alexandria was celebrated in February 1821. Mohammed Ali Pasha was greatly relieved from this work (and it was named Mahmoudieh after the reigning Sultan).

Pascal Coste, Mohamed Ali's Chief Engineer, in *Tārīkh khalīj al-Iskandarīyah al-qadīm wa-tur'at al- Maḥmūdīyah* by Prince Omar Toussoun, 1942.

The Mahmoudieh Canal, 1890.

The Mahmoudieh Canal

It was cut, by command of Mehemet Ali, in the year 1819, the destruction of the old one, 18 years previously, having ruined Alexandrian trade by isolating the city from the grand old river. After the death of Sir Ralph Abercrombie, when the British were trying to dislodge the French troops from Alexandria, they cut great sluices in the banks of the canal near Damietta, intending thereby to cut off the garrison from communication with the rest of Egypt, as also to stop the supply of fresh water. In the rush which ensued the waters of the Lake Aboukir were drained down to the ancient bed of the Lake Mareotis, producing a vast inundation to the east and south of the city—a new feature in the country, which the French soon turned to their advantage, bringing a flotilla of gun-boats to work on this newly created sea. So the Pasha very wisely determined to make a new canal; but he showed neither wisdom nor mercy in the way he set about it. Vast multitudes of those poor, hard-worked, and much-oppressed fellahs, about whom we have lately heard so much, were gathered together—250,000 men, women and children, half naked, were forced to work in the burning sun, under command of brutal task-masters, who, as in the days of Pharaoh, did not hesitate freely to use their scourge of cords to encourage the weary. Not the men only, but women and little children, were lashed until they literally streamed with blood. No regular tools were provided: each brought his own poor basket of palm leaves to carry away the sand and mud, which they scooped with their hands. No wages were given, and only the most miserable food; so it was small wonder that, by the very lowest computation, 23,000 of these poor wretches perished from starvation, disease, and exhaustion. Their bodies being shoveled in with the sand and mud, helped to raise the canal banks, making them at the same time into a horrible, ghastly cemetery. But the 50 miles of canal were completed in one year, (some accounts say in six weeks!) and human life in Egypt is of small importance when balanced against a great man's will.

Gentleman's Magazine, The New York Times, August 20, 1882.

CANAL MAHMOUDIEH A ALEXANDRIE

S.I.P

The Mahmoudieh Canal. "Mohamed Ali arranged for the repair and cleaning of the canal supplying fresh water to Alexandria and providing a waterway connection with the interior. Without this canal and access to its safe drinking water, the city of Alexandria could not have existed." —Sandro Breccia, *The Port of Alexandria*, 1926.

The Mahmoudieh Canal. "With its cool waters and its shade, the magnificent villas gracing its banks, and the superb gardens which delight the eye, the canal is an enormously popular place for excursions and pleasant walks. This canal is constantly full of boats of all shapes, including the dahabiyeh, an elegant and charming house-boat, found only in the Orient." —E. François-Levernay, *Directory of Egypt for the year 1872–1873*.

368. *Alexandrien, Mahmudieh Kanal*
Alexandria, The Mamudieh Canal

The Mahmoudieh Canal. "Restaurants and dairies are to be found along the whole length of the canal." —E. François-Levernay, *Directory of Egypt for the year 1872–1873.*

The Bourse of Minet-el-Bassal

Silvio Pinto

1935

In October 1933, the Bourse of Minet el-Bassal Company celebrated its fiftieth anniversary. The event passed unnoticed by many and would have escaped me had I not signed the report of the shareholders' 50th General Assembly as President of the company which manages the Bourse.

The building of Minet el-Bassal Bourse was constructed by the Grand Khedive Ismail I, but it was difficult to find the exact year. In a publication at the Municipal Library, a certain Vernay wrote under the title "Alexandria in 1872": "In the Minet el-Bassal district, a Bourse of commerce is being built at the expense of His Highness the Khedive." At the time, almost all of the cotton belonged to the Viceroy and, according to the same author, there were 200,000 inhabitants in the city of Alexandria, and barely 5,000,000 in the whole of Egypt.

In Arabic Minet el-Bassal means "Port of Onions". This applies to the entire district, home, for a long time, to the onion trade. It is bizarre that today the place of cotton and cottonseed is called "Port of Onions"; it should be called "Minet el-Aktan" or "Port of Cotton", or to be more precise, "the Bourse of Cotton in the district of Minet el-Bassal".

According to the Commission of State Domains from which the Bourse of Minet el-Bassal was bought, in 1878 a decree by Ismail relinquished to the State all the khedivial family's real estate, under a Commission of Domains, composed of an Egyptian, an Englishman and a Frenchman.

In the same report we find: on 1 September 1879 a mortgage contract for a building in Minet el-Bassal as guarantee for the loan of 8.5 million pounds, and on 18 October 1882 a letter from the Commissioners to the President of the Council and to Messrs. Rothschild, concerning the loss of the pledge resulting from a fire in the Alexandria buildings. The Commission adds: "All that the Commission of Domains is left with is the Bourse of Minet-el-Bassal and a house in Porte Rosette." Isn't it curious that all the buildings pledged to the Rothschilds had been destroyed by the fires during the events of 1882, except for two, one of which is the Bourse of Minet-el-Bassal?

In the Commission of Domains report we read: "Various circumstances forced us to cede the Bourse of Minet el-Bassal at an inferior price to what it had cost." Already at that time, we can see that Alexandrian merchants were used to making good deals.

The bill of sale, dated 6 July 1885, shows the release from mortgage of Messrs. Rothschild Brothers of Paris and Messrs. Rothschild Sons of London.

On the list of Alexandria merchants, on whose behalf Messrs. Birch, Benachi and Goussio conducted the purchase, we find the names of commercial establishments that still exist today, such as Peel, Behrend, Choremi Benachi, Planta, Carver and Rolo.

"The bill of sale informs the purchasers that it pays a monthly bond of around P.T. 100 for the maintenance and care of the tomb of a holy man called Sheikh Abdel Kader, built in the room N.E. of the crates pavilion, and that it allows on some days of the year free access to those who wish to practice their devotion. It transmits this constraint to the purchasers, the same way it received and respected it itself, despite it not being mentioned in the budgets."

The company continues to respect this constraint and the descendant heirs of the Sheikh still have the privilege of free access to the Bourse to worship; moreover, every devout Muslim who is at the Bourse doesn't fail to go every day to the Sheikh's tomb to say a prayer. This peculiarity, a place of devotion within the walls of a bourse, the

Share of the Société Egyptienne de la Bourse Commerciale de Minet el-Bassal, 1923.

contrast of the sacred and the secular, is always strongly noticed by foreign visitors.

The current Bourse stretches over a surface of approximately 9,400 m², demarcated by four big streets. On the ground floor, sixty-eight offices are all rented to exporters or cotton traders, except for one reserved for the Post Office, Telegraph and Telephone and two occupied by cafeterias. A big room assigned to the Bourse Committee meetings is on the ground floor. On the first floor, four big offices are rented to the Commission of the Bourse where cotton evaluations and bids are made, an office is reserved for the Government's Commissioner at the Bourse, another one is occupied by the Government Statistics office. Some rooms are rented to the Testing House, the institution in charge of the cotton hygrometric test, in case of dispute.

Three *chounehs* [warehouses] with a total surface of around 5,000 m² complete this enormous building that is the center of Egyptian cotton works. The *chounehs* were rebuilt in 1917 and a first floor was added, but several more construction and reconstructions were made to accommodate the ever-increasing number of cotton establishments. In 1906, eight new offices were built. In 1907 a floor was built above the offices located in the center of the Bourse, and in 1910, again three new offices.

The room reserved for the Board of Directors' meetings, later assigned to the Alexandria General Produce Association meetings, then to the Bourse of Minet el-Bassal Commission which succeeded it was built in 1910. Three years later, automatic fire extinguishers were installed throughout the Bourse, and in 1914, four new offices were built.

In 1917, part of the *chounehs* were relinquished to make twenty new offices on the ground floor. These last constructions were made at a time when the price of materials was very high, but it was impossible for the Board of Directors to shirk its duty to satisfy all the new exporters clamouring for offices on the ground floor.

The Company of the Bourse, despite the privilege granted to it by the government in 1884 for a period of ninety-nine years, has kept rents and rights of access to the Bourse within reasonable limits and has always sought to satisfy all interested parties as much as possible. The maximum rent of an office is L.E. 150 annually, including free entry for ten employees. The right of access to the Bourse for those who do not have an office varies from L.E. 1 to 4 per year, depending on the subscriber's category.

Before the other war, no fees were collected to enter the Bourse although a paid subscription had been planned. But then, such things were disregarded, the whole world was less formal and more *bon enfant*. The number of subscription cards is currently 805 and that of free access for tenants and employees is 50. There are 25 free access cards for Government officials and journalists. The total is 1,580. To this, it is necessary to add about a hundred more for sample carriers, office and Bourse domestics, who have free access with a plate showing the name of the company that employs them. They must wear this plate clearly on the arm or on the chest.

When we think that in 1863–64 the total export of Egyptian cotton was only 150,000 bales and that in 1933–34 it reached about 1 million bales, we can see the development of cotton culture and trade in Egypt and, consequently, the importance acquired by the Bourse of Minet el-Bassal.

And finally, I will point out a few singularities, some disappeared, like the two basins in the central courtyard, with their aquatic plants and goldfish; the colourful seller of the famous *arghissous* drink; the Turkish seller of so-called Persian carpets; the old porter that people back then nicknamed "Cadorna", a mustachioed caricature that would

Alexandrie   Bourse de Minet el Bassal

The Bourse of Minet-el-Bassal, Alexandria's Cotton Exchange. Postcard dated 1903.

make any Montenegrin *kawas* pale, tasseled and adorned, dragging an immense saber, nostalgia, no doubt, for when he had been a non-commissioned police officer, of which he kept a martial appearance and several decorations. While all this only remains in the memory of a few, we still have a seller of mocha coffee who continues to grind his coffee in his shop—a trade passed down from father to son—a very good coffee, appreciated by lovers of this drink, in the café of Minet el-Bassal. What no longer exists and added to the local colour is the *nargileh*, very in vogue then, not only among Egyptians, but also among Europeans.

In short, thirty or forty years ago, entering the Bourse, one had the impression of a calm and "oriental machismo." Today the impression is quite different, even opposite: that of western energy. No trace of those fish-containing basins, nor of the *nargileh* smoker, but struggling brokers, sweaty sample porters, people who come and go, all very busy or pretending to be.

The poet prefers past times, but the hectic modern life, does not adapt well to poetry.

La Reforme, Golden Edition, 1945.

Insurance plan of Minet el Bassal, 1880.

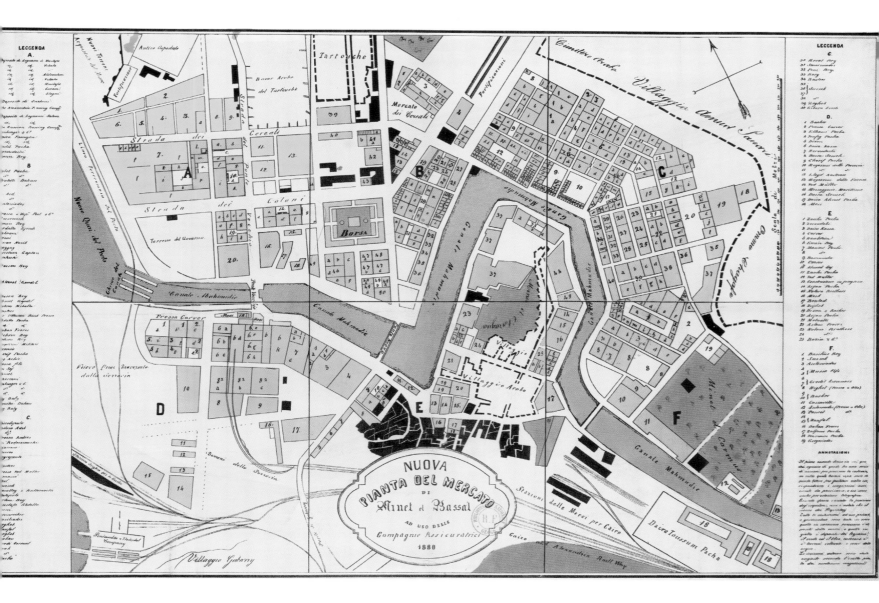

NUOVA
PIANTA DEL MERCATO
DI
Minet el Bassal
AD USO DELLE
Compagnie Assicuratrici
1880

Rue du Gabbari.

ALEXANDRIE. MOSQUE A GABARI.

Gabbari Mosque, named after Abu el-Kassem el-Gabbari bin Mansour bin Yehia, a Sufi ascetic born circa 1229 and said to be buried here

Le Palais de S. A. le Khédive Saïd Pacha au Mez

Alexandrie

44 Made for Pierre Agopian, Alexandria, Egypt.

The palace of Saïd Pasha (Viceroy 1854–1863) in Mex. In addition to his Kasr el-Nil palace in Cairo, Saïd Pasha built a palace in Gabbari and one in Mex which was never completed. By 1878, it was a "bulbous ruin".

209. - ALEXANDRIE. - Phare du Mex

The Mex Lighthouse. Postcard dated 1902.

No. 36. **Alexandrie**   Les forts et village du Mex.

The forts and village of Mex. *Mex* is the singular of *mokkous*, a tax levied on merchants on entry to Alexandria from the west.

The semaphore of Mex.

The Catacombs

In imitation of the ancient Egyptians, the Greeks who ruled Alexandria, and after them the Christians, buried their dead in graves hollowed out from solid rock. Here as everywhere, the necropolis was to the west of the city, facing the setting sun, the tombs marking the end of life, as the sunset marks the end of the day. This necropolis stretched from the sea to Lake Mareotis. Important remains are to be found along the seashore, between the Cairo railway station and the outskirts of Mex; more are also to be found near the Mahmoudieh Canal, at a place called Karmouz. The former are more important; they allow us to visualise a multiplicity of chambers lined with two, three or four rows of tombs of different size, connected to each other by direct passageways or by stairs, all cut into a soft limestone rock which was quickly eroded by the sea air and humidity; which explains how these pillars and columns weakened to the point where, no longer able to bear the enormous weight of the vaults, everything slowly crumbled to form an immense and shapeless mass of rubble which then vanished only to reappear as part of new construction. Some of the tombs are submerged, which can only be explained in three ways: the rock face which protected them from the sea has disappeared, eroded by the waves; or, as a result of some natural disaster, the level of the ground has been lowered; or else the level of the sea has risen.

The first hypothesis seems to us the most correct, since a certain number of chambers, popularly called bathing chambers, are connected to the sea by means of gullies made by human hand, which bring water into one side of the chamber and return it to the sea on the other side. They have the appearance of lustration chambers where corpses were washed prior to burial. Other excavations, also classed as catacombs, are found to the southwest of Pompey's Column, near the Mahmoudieh Canal, behind the Antoniadis olive oil mill.

On the walls of the twenty-three-step staircase descending to a small platform open to the sky, it is still possible even today to see some primitive paintings representing saints and attributes of Christianity, their Greek inscriptions largely erased; the remains of an altar carved into the soft rock; a gallery 12 metres long displaying two rows of niches; and part of a cistern. Several steps down from this point is a doorway, recently blocked, but formerly the entrance to a series of large galleries extending as far as Pompey's Column. Prohibiting the use of this entrance was a wise decision since landslides and accidents have occurred in these underground passages.

E. François-Levernay, *Directory of Egypt for the year 1872–1873.*

The Catacombs of Mex, circa 1890.

On The Currently Closed Bourse

Jules Klat

1945

The War brought, among other upheavals, the closure of our Merchandise Bourse. For Egypt, more than elsewhere, the Bourse will remain the base of its economic structure and as soon as the world returns to normalcy, the Bourse will emerge to regain its leading place in this country.

Our Cotton Bourse has been closed since 13 May, 1940. For more than four years, we no longer hear the clamour of the trading floor, nor the echoes of feverish activity transmitted to all corners of Egypt and the world. Fluctuations in cotton price occupy first place everywhere in Egypt. We see them posted day and night in all establishments eager to meet the information needs of their customers.

For several years Reuters has been operating the "ticker" in Egypt, the introduction of which I greatly encouraged. Thanks to a transmission device installed at the Bourse in a small cabin overlooking the floor, prices are instantly known throughout Egypt instead of slow transmission by telephone and telegram.

Since the closure of the Bourse, the ticker operator's cabin has been vacant and silence hangs over the cotton trading floor where hundreds once swarmed. Something is amiss in the commercial life of Alexandria and all of Egypt. It would have been difficult to imagine that Egypt, whose main product is cotton, could remain so long without the organism regulating its flow.

It was created in 1861 when some brokers in Alexandria established the first futures market for cotton and cereals in a place on the street still called Rue de l'Ancienne Bourse.

Following a discord, dissident brokers created a second cotton bourse at the present location of the Cook agency, Fouad I Street. For a while the two operated simultaneously, resulting in different prices for the same commodity at the same time.

The abnormal situation lasted only a few months, and in 1889 twenty-five brokers formed the Association of Commodity Brokers which is the origin of the current Bourse. The association held its meetings in the current premises of the Bourse, formerly held by a limited company. The building is now owned by the Municipality. It is in a state of dilapidation but we still have hope the future Palais de la Bourse will be part of the Boulevard Ismail, a grandiose project we have heard about for so long which our children may one day see.

Operations were formerly carried out in Italian, at the time the language used in commercial transactions and in the courts.

The futures market operated in Alexandria without government interference until 1909, when it was regulated by law.

Since then Bourse operations have enjoyed the protection of the Courts. A forward transaction is now valid regardless of the parties intentions as to its outcome and without the judge having to determine whether the operation should be settled by delivery of the goods or simple settlement of price difference.

In Egypt, the broker profession is free. It suffices to fulfill certain conditions of morality, internship and capital. Admission is subject to a secret ballot by members of the Commission, with the right to appeal before the Courts. Regulation provides for summoning the President of the Commission before the Court to give the reasons why a candidate is rejected, while the decision was taken by secret ballot. We can understand the embarrassment of the President of the Commission called to provide in court and in the presence of the interested party the reasons, almost always of a moral nature, which motivated the refusal and whose proof is most often impossible to prove.

The rules of the Bourse have undergone numerous amendments and changes. Each amendment has its history and is subjected to preliminary studies, deliberations, general assemblies and sometimes conflicts with the Government. Often a deleted or amended measure is reinstated after an unsuccessful experience, as was the case with the dealers who were laid off at the request of the Government and were subsequently reinstated.

In Alexandria, the President of the Bourse is elected each year and is always eligible for re-election. Here are the names of those who have assumed this function since the Bourse regulation by the Government:

Ibr. Arab in 1911.
A. Gandour 1912–1921.
G. Caralli 1922–1924.
Jules Klat Bey 1924–1945.

During many crises, managers of the Bourse were often brought to take exceptional measures to avoid or reduce disturbances. These measures, such as the collective suspension of jobbers and the provisional fixing of minimum and maximum prices, aim at reducing speculation and artificially limiting fluctuation.

Thanks to the control the Bourse Commission exercises over its members and in particular mandatory verification of capital and positions of each agency, our Bourse has been able to overcome the turmoil of these past few years without any defaults. Our Bourse could have been an example to world Bourses were it not for the compulsory closing imposed in 1940.

At the time, the Government became buyer of any quantity of cotton offered at a fixed price. The Mediterranean blockade stopped all exports and made the Government buyer of the entire crop. A decree ordered the closure of the Bourse and the obligatory compensation of all positions.

It was the most serious measure our Bourse has endured, causing immense damage to many trading houses and the forced unemployment of several hundred people.

I cannot but compare these events with the arrangements made during the other Great War. The Bourse Commission at the time, panicking at the declaration of war, had ordered compulsory compensation for positions in cotton and cereals. But the Government, by decree, cancelled compensation, restoring the closed positions. It also suspended the Bourse Commission and entrusted its functions to a Government Commission.

Since the Bourse closed, first an Anglo-Egyptian Commission then an Egyptian Commission were created to buy the cotton crop and ensure the country's finances. They made their purchases outside Bourse brokers, who were kept unemployed. These Commissions made several million pounds of profit. But there were no allowances to compensate, as in Liverpool, those who have seen their professional activity suspended. The Bourse Commission was only authorised to contract a loan repayable upon the reopening of the Bourse by taxes on their future profits.

Let us hope this will not be delayed long and that in the near future the Bourse will resume its essential function in a better world.

La Reforme, Golden Edition, 1945.

The Cotton Barons of Alexandria

La Reforme

1945

Oswald Finney

Oswald James Finney, a true "Anglo-Egyptian", was born in Alexandria on 20 February 1880. His father was a partner in Carver Bros. and Gill, a leading cotton trade firm. He left Egypt in 1881 for health reasons and returned to England but spent the winter in San Remo. Due to his frequent stays on the Riviera, his son Oswald learned perfect French and Italian and had a keen interest in art.

At the age of eighteen, after he received the Oxford and Cambridge Higher Certificate, Oswald Finney apprenticed at Reynolds and Gibson, one of Liverpool's main cotton agents. But he wished to return to Alexandria. When he came of age, he worked for Carver Bros. for three years, then at Mallison and Co. as a cotton expert.

In 1908, when Mr. Reinhart founded his export company, Finney managed his cotton branch. In a few years, it was a leading Alexandrian exporter.

In 1915, he left Reinhart to become managing director of the Alexandria Cotton Co. Two years later, he founded The Commercial Co. of Egypt, and, in 1923, the Alexandria Commercial Co., where he remained President until his death.

The Alexandria Commercial Co. was an immediate success. He also established a yeast factory, a pressing and ginning factory and real estate and insurance companies. Financial companies asked him to sit on their board.

By 1926, he owned the Société Orientale de Publicité, which in addition to advertising, owned three newspapers—*La Bourse Egyptienne d'Alexandrie, La Bourse Egyptienne du Caire* and the *Egyptian Mail*—and a specialized magazine, *La Presse Medicale d'Egypte*. Finney added *La Revue d'Egypte Economique et Financière*, the *Egyptian Gazette,* the *Progrès Egyptien*, and *The Sphinx*.

His generous donations to el-Moassat Hospital earned him national recognition. He was a benefactor of el-Orwah el-Woska, the Société de Bienfaisance Copte, the British Benevolent Fund and city hospitals. The Minet el-Bassal clinic was his initiative.

Before his marriage in 1912, he shared an apartment with friends overlooking the Alexandria Cricket Club. He bought the property and transformed it into a private mansion decorated in Venetian style. His collections include jade; enamels from Chelsea, Crown Derby, and Canton; remarkable Dresden porcelain; tapestries by Gobelins; and paintings by masters.

From 1922 to 1926, he sat on the Alexandria Municipal Council. He founded the Union Alexandrine, a group of notables who fended for the city.

Three months after his death, the Alexandria Municipality held a memorial ceremony, the first time in its history, attended by President of the Council, the Governor, the Director General of the Municipality and the city elite.

Alfred Reinhart

Reinhart and Co., a Swiss merchant firm in Alexandria, was founded in 1907 by Alfred Reinhart.

The Reinhart family was in the cotton trade since the middle of the nineteenth century. Johann Caspar Reinhart, head of Geilinger & Blum in Winterthur, Switzerland, traded in cotton from Macedonia and the United States. He sent his son Paul to Alexandria in 1858, where he was a founding member of the Swiss Society of Alexandria, returning home

USE EGYPT'S FAMOUS LONG - STAPLE COTTON FOR HIGH QUALITY
COTTON TEXTILES

Advertisement illustrating the many uses of cotton, in *Egypt Today*, 1939.

to develop the import of Egyptian cotton in Switzerland and surrounding countries.

His brother Louis was established in Le Hâvre, France where he became one of the largest cotton importers. Another brother, Théodore, married the daughter of one of the founders of the Volkart Bros. who developed the cotton trade with India. His sons and grandson head the world-renowned firm Volkart Bros.

In 1893, Geilinger & Blum became Paul Reinhart and Cie. and had become general agents for Europe, including Russia, major cotton exporters of American cotton. He assigned his two sons Paul Junior and Alfred to careers in the cotton trade. They underwent severe but useful internships first with their uncle at Le Havre, then in England and in the United States. Paul Junior became a partner in his father's company while Alfred went to Egypt.

Alfred Reinhart arrived in Alexandria in 1896. He started working at the F. C. Baines & Co., a cotton export firm and soon became a partner. In 1907 Reinhart founded his own firm, Reinhart and Co. A year later, it became an English limited company, with two major American and English cotton merchants as partners. Reinhart directed the firm and maintained it during the war (1914–1918) as one of the most important exporters. Shortly after the war, Reinhart returned it to a limited partnership; he founded Reinhart and Gilg in Manchester and Reinhart and Co. Inc. in Boston, Massachusetts, and established a close liaison with Paul Reinhart and Cie. in Switzerland.

J. Planta & Co.

Pierre de Planta was born 3 April 3 1829 in Dusch, the canton of Graubünden, Switzerland. After completing studies in Switzerland, an internship in a trading firm in Basel, and professional training in a cotton mill in northern Italy then at an export firm in Trieste, he came to Egypt in 1853 where he founded, with his cousin Jacques, J. &

P. Planta, Commercial Register Nº 1, Alexandria. He died in Switzerland in 1911 at the age of 82. One of his sons, François de Planta, took over the management of J. Planta and Co.

This old cotton export firm, the doyenne of Swiss firms in the industry, was founded in 1853 and is also one of the oldest and most important in the Alexandria. It started when Egypt produced 300,000 to 500,000 cantars of cotton. Then, J. & P. Planta mainly exported cereals, beans, flax, sugar, and ivory and arabic gum from Sudan. It imported iron, sheets and porcelain from England, wood from Trieste and glassworks from Belgium.

De Planta claim the pioneering role of introducing mechanical ginning in Egypt. Until then, cotton ginning was done by hand. The imperfections, the slowness, and especially the lack of purity were disconcerting. Soon, steam powered a factory with forty looms, and a pure cotton that was commercially classified and consistent having finally been produced, factories were set up in Tanta, Mansoura and Zagazig.

With cotton as the firm's main product, it opened agencies and sub-agencies to purchase it, with a system of cash advances to cultivators and sellers. When the American Civil War broke out in 1861, circumstances converged to place it at the top.

Cotton was then treated only after it was harvested and paid for in cash, sometimes at great risk to the merchant. Farmers, eager to augment profits because of the American Civil War, increased production, which was agreeable with the consumer-spinners who had adopted Egyptian cotton. But in 1862 when prices rose to $30, domestic traders, mostly Greek, seeing the inevitable end of hostilities, sought relief of their commitments through delivery by contract. Traders believed de Planta would keep their word regardless of fluctuations. Spinners, on the other hand, wanted the goods at the price of the day. The firm

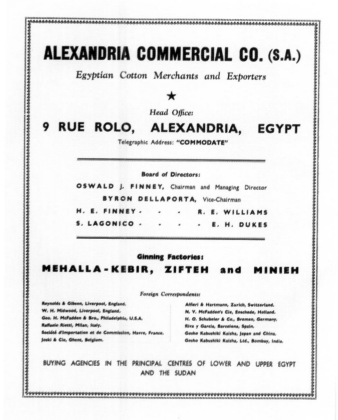

ALEXANDRIA COMMERCIAL CO. (S.A.)

Egyptian Cotton Merchants and Exporters

★

Head Office:

9 RUE ROLO, ALEXANDRIA, EGYPT

Telegraphic Address: "COMMODATE"

Board of Directors:

OSWALD J. FINNEY, *Chairman and Managing Director*

BYRON DELLAPORTA, *Vice-Chairman*

H. E. FINNEY   -   R. E. WILLIAMS

S. LAGONICO   -   E. H. DUKES

Ginning Factories:

MEHALLA - KEBIR, ZIFTEH and MINIEH

Foreign Correspondents:

Reynolds & Gibson, Liverpool, England.
W. H. Midwood, Liverpool, England.
Geo. H. McFadden & Bro., Philadelphia, U.S.A.
Raffaele Rietti, Milan, Italy.
Société d'Importation et de Commission, Havre, France.
Joski & Cie, Ghent, Belgium.

Alfieri & Hartmann, Zurich, Switzerland.
N. V. McFadden's Cie, Enschede, Holland.
H. O. Schubeler & Co., Bremen, Germany.
Riva y Garcia, Barcelona, Spain.
Gosho Kabushiki Kaisha, Japan and China.
Gosho Kabushiki Kaisha, Ltd., Bombay, India.

BUYING AGENCIES IN THE PRINCIPAL CENTRES OF LOWER AND UPPER EGYPT AND THE SUDAN

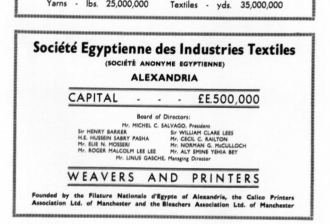

FILATURE NATIONALE D'EGYPTE

SOCIÉTÉ ANONYME EGYPTIENNE

Established in 1911

ALEXANDRIA

Capital - - £500,000

Board of Directors:

Mr. MICHEL C. SALVAGO, President

Sir HENRY BARKER	Mr. A. J. LOWE
Mr. OSWALD J. FINNEY	Mr. RAPHAEL TORIEL
Mr. ELIE N. MOSSERI	Mr. C. M. SALVAGO
Mr. N. G. McCULLOCH	Mr. ALY EMINE YEHIA BEY

Mr. LINUS GASCHE, Managing Director

SPINNERS, WEAVERS, BLEACHERS AND DYERS

Annual Production:

Yarns - lbs. 25,000,000   Textiles - yds. 35,000,000

Société Egyptienne des Industries Textiles

(SOCIÉTÉ ANONYME EGYPTIENNE)

ALEXANDRIA

CAPITAL - - - £E.500,000

Board of Directors:

Mr. MICHEL C. SALVAGO, President

Sir HENRY BARKER	Sir WILLIAM CLARE LEES
H.E. HUSSEIN SABRY PASHA	Mr. CECIL C. RAILTON
Mr. ELIE N. MOSSERI	Mr. NORMAN G. McCULLOCH
Mr. ROGER MALCOLM LEE LEE	Mr. ALY EMINE YEHIA BEY

Mr. LINUS GASCHE, Managing Director

WEAVERS AND PRINTERS

Founded by the Filature Nationale d'Egypte of Alexandria, the Calico Printers Association Ltd. of Manchester and the Bleachers Association Ltd. of Manchester

Advertisements in *Egypt Today*, 1939.

developed a genre that, combined with turnover, was equivalent to hedging and met the needs of both spinners and interior traders. It was the only firm to offer this work based on the trust it enjoyed with its domestic counterpart.

Choremi Benachi Cotton Co.

Choremi, Mellor & Co. was founded in 1858 by Messrs. Jean Choremi and Mellor to buy cotton in Egypt and sell it in Liverpool, with headquarters in Alexandria and a branch in Liverpool under the name of Mellor & Co.

In 1876, when Jean Choremi and Mellor left the business, the company was renamed Choremi, Benachi & Co. The main partners were Emmanuil A. Benachi, brother-in-law of Jean Choremi, Lucas A. Benachi, his brother, Demosthènes Choremi, the brother of Jean Choremi, and Thomas Davies. An affiliate was established in Liverpool under the name of Davies, Benachi & Co.

Later, they were successively replaced by Constantin J. Choremi, Antoine E. Benachi, Alexandre E. Benachi, Etienne Delta, Antoine L. Benachi, Auguste Th. Sinadino, John Hampson Lloyd, JP Jones, Colonel John E. Lloyd, Alexandre L. Benachi, and Thomas E. H. Davies. It was not until the death of Constantin J. Choremi, senior partner in 1935, that it became the Choremi Benachi Cotton Co. S.A.E.

Upon the death of Colonel John E. Lloyd in 1941, the presidency was entrusted to Auguste Sinadino.

Davies, Benachi & Co. continued to represent Choremi Benachi Cotton Co. S.A.E. in the United Kingdom with headquarters in Liverpool.

Choremi, Benachi & Co. was closely linked to the development of the cotton trade and industry in Egypt, with agencies and sub-agencies in the important centres of cotton production and ginning factories in Upper and Lower Egypt.

Choremi, Benachi & Co. encouraged cotton seed selection and contributed to the introduction of the new qualities which consolidated the reputation of Egyptian cotton and expanded its consumption throughout the world.

Choremi, Benachi & Co. maintained a team of renowned cotton experts, technicians in its factories and workshops, personnel in its administration and various offices, and hundreds of workers in its factories.

The founders and administrators of Choremi, Benachi & Co. sit on the boards of the main financial establishments, industries, and public utilities, the association committees, commissions of the cotton trade, as well as the cotton and economic commissions of the Egyptian Government.

Choremi, Benachi & Co. also represented insurance companies such as Reliance Marine Insurance Co. in Liverpool, and Prudential Assurance Company in London.

Mohamed Farghali Pasha

Mohamed Farghali Pasha went to university in Egypt then London where he obtained the higher certificate of Oxford and Cambridge. Upon his return, he joined his father's firm which was founded in 1865 and whom he succeeded.

Farghali Pasha is Chairman of Presses Libres Egyptiennes and La Fluviale S.A.E. He is President of the Lower Egypt Ginning Pool and the Alexandria Cotton Exporters Association. He sits on the Board of Directors of National Bank of Egypt; Misr Company for Spinning and Weaving, Mahalla; Misr Company for Spinning and Weaving of Fine Cotton, Kafr and Dawar; Beida Dyers S.A.E.; The Land Bank of Egypt; The Associated Cotton Ginners of Egypt; Rosetta & Alexandria Rice Mills Co.; Alexandria Credit Company; Immobilia S.A.E.; The Gabbari Land Co.; Misr Insurance Company; Misr Maritime Navigation

Advertisement in *Egypt Today*, 1939.

Company; The Upper Egypt Ginning Co.; Textile Fibers Industry; Egyptian Finance Company for Trade & Industry; La Gérance Immobilière; S.A. des bières Bomonti & Pyramids; California Texas Petroleum Company; Bata S.A.E.; The New Egyptian Co Ltd.; Tramways d'Alexandrie; The Trading Corporation of Egypt; Misr Aviation Company; Marconi Radio & Telegram Co. Ltd.; Société Texas Eygptienne des Pétroles; Société California Egyptienne des Pétroles.

Farghali Pasha was a senator in 1943, a member of the Municipal Council, President of the Cotton Exporters Union, a prominent Rotarian and a socialite. An accomplished turfman, his colours are among the most popular on the racetracks of Cairo and Alexandria.

Levy Rossano & Co.

Founded by Robert Levy and Charles Rossano who tenaciously managed to break into the club of pioneer cotton exporters, such as the Peels, the Carvers, the Choremis, the Salvagos, the Toriels, and the Addàs.

To achieve his goal, Robert Levy put to use his keen sense of business, a solid experience, a remarkable sense of organization and an intelligence that clarified the most difficult problems.

Charles Rossano brought the enthusiasm of youthful passion, an intuition seldom wrong, an extraordinary memory and a technique that all Minet el-Bassal recognizes—the art of making friends everywhere. He established personal contacts on the Continent, in England, in India. His way of doing business and good humour were appreciated everywhere.

The year the company was founded, its exports amounted to 3,500 bales; in 1932–33, they rose to 18,800 bales; in 1935–36 they were already at 42,900; they climbed to 56,500 in 1936–37, peaking at 60,200 in 1937–38 on the eve of the war.

In 1940, Robert Levy died. Shaken for a moment by the blow, Charles Rossano soon recovered and continued the work. Levy Rossano and Co. remains a success story.

Pinto Cotton Company

Pinto Cotton Co. S.A.E is one of the most important cotton buying and exporting firms in Egypt. It replaced Pinto and Co. founded in 1911 by Silvio Pinto with his father as partner and sponsor, the late I.O. Pinto. Since then, it included among its associates and members, the brothers of Silvio Pinto: Attilio Pinto, Ezio Pinto and the late Edgardo Pinto.

Pinto and Co. always dealt in cotton, the foundation of Egypt's wealth: the acquisition of cotton and its seed, ginning, and exporting constituted most of its activities.

Pinto and Co. became one of the main cotton export companies with a total load of 45,356 bales for the year 1938–39. That year, it ranked third in exports to Great Britain with total shipments of 25,266 bales.

Edwin N. Goar

As soon as he finished his studies at the age of 17, Edwin Goar joined his father at Naggiar, Goar, Levi & Co., later dissolved and replaced by Joseph Goar & Son. On the death of his father in 1909, the young Goar took over the company which reached great prosperity.

It is active in the export of cotton seed and in the import of coal; flour; raw silk from India, China, Italy and France; rice and sacks from India; Java sugar; Ceylon tea; not to mention the cotton trade within Egypt and administering its vast agricultural estates and real estate.

Edwin Goar is President of the Cotton Seed Committee, former President of the Import Trade, President of the Export Trade Association, member of the Minet el-Bassal Bourse Commission, and former member of the Municipal Council, member of the Board of Directors of Alexandria Insurance Company and of Alexandria Life Insurance.

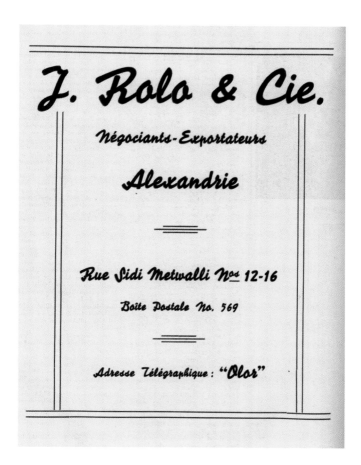

Advertisement in *La Reforme*, 1945.

He donated land to Victoria College, which made it the largest and the best fitted in Egypt and the Middle East. He is the governor of Victoria College and member of the Board of Directors of the British Boys School and the English Girls College.

He is Vice-President of the Israelite Community Council, President of Amélé-Torah, the school aid for food and clothing, administrator of the Great Temple Eliahou-Hannabi, former Honorary Treasurer for fifteen years of the International Bureau for the Protection of Women and Girls, member of the Social Alliance and of el-Mobarra Committee created by the Governor of Alexandria to help the poor people of the city, and member of the Central Committee of the Egyptian Red Crescent.

His son and main collaborator, Gustave Goar, volunteered at the start of the war as Fl. Lt. at the Royal Air Force. His grandson Philip enlisted in the Royal Air Force.

Advertisement in *Egypt Today*, 1939.

Alexandria, Gate of the West

Fernand Leprette

1940

Minet el-Bassal: the palace of King Cotton. It is certainly not beautiful. It is a bare, yellowish, leprous cube, surrounded by high railings through which small, badly tied up parcels, their tow stuffing peering out, can be seen piled up on dirty shelves. In this thickly populated, sordid district, on the edge of the Mahmoudieh Canal, this building is only distinguishable by its shabby, untidy aspect from the numerous outhouses, warehouses and *chounehs*. A casual passerby would never imagine it to be the temple of the wealth of Egypt, were it not, perhaps, for the row of Chryslers, Buicks and Packards, great petrol consumers, whose chauffeurs are always busy polishing the mirrors and varnishing as they cover with the same fluff dust.

From Gabbari bridge and all the neighbouring streets arises the clatter of enormous trucks with their wobbly bales, and rumbling sledges pushed through a grey mist by barefooted workmen. At the *chouneh* doors, Roman weighing machines stand in their tripods. A bale, like an enormous block of the Pyramids, is lifted up in obedience to a sign from the man in charge who, realizing the importance of his task, pushes his heavy slide along the beam: 400, 410, 420 kilos.

With a firm hand he paints a few numbers on the jute envelope and copies them down in a notebook. The bale is then hauled up the side of a wall and disappears through a hole into which it is dragged by a multitude of arms. Meanwhile, carts continue their mad race round the outside of the palace, going backwards and forwards between the boats at Gabbari, the storehouse district and, thence, tired of their long circumnavigation, to the maritime quays. The noise and bustle, even greater than in the harbour, is quite deafening.

Not everyone is allowed in this temple, although you may be invited by these gentlemen. The President, to whom a well-known Parisian writer (who has lived in Egypt for fifteen years) is introduced, must first offer you a cup of coffee or, in other words, add his *sta bene* to your visit. Everyone is extremely polite but a certain ceremonial must be gone through. Your friend the broker introduces you to his boss from the National Bank, a cheery, dark, red-faced Englishman who also offers you a cup of coffee. "This is a den of thieves," he tells you confidentially, "and your friend is the most dangerous of them all." This den is a sunny courtyard but such is the humour of the place. It would be a great mistake to imagine that this crowd, among which very few tarbouches are seen, is idle, as would appear on a first impression. Beneath the jovial manner there is a certain way of instantly clinching a deal with a joke and a slap over the shoulder. As with the town gossips, you have to understand the most fleeting allusions and juggle with a notebook and pencil. You are surrounded by conjurers: an egg, a rabbit, a top hat and the result is an order. It is all part of the game.

What is this famous palace like? An open courtyard surrounded by tiny cells, bearing plain copper plates: on one side the importers, on the other side the exporters. Between 11 a.m. and 1 p.m., four, five or six thousand bales of cotton pass through here daily, and, after a holiday, sometimes as many as 200,000 which represents the sum of L.E. 400,000. All you see of this cotton is the parcels containing specimen of the qualities supplied by the various firms and the patterns brought from the storehouses in jute envelopes. Still, the air is full of cotton. You see it between everyone's fingers, in front of their eyes and in their thoughts. "All the wealth of Egypt," as they say with complacent pride.

A man in an unbleached linen suit enters one of the cells, comes out again and disappears into the one next door like a bee gathering honey.

Mohamed Ali Square, circa 1934.

He is a broker. A large black table in front of a wide bay window, a few parcels on the shelves, a telephone in a corner and, perhaps, a chair. There is no question of comfort here but of wealth, or rather business. A smartly dressed gentleman has rolled up the sleeves of his silk shirt: he is the classifier of an export firm. He asks for a specimen of the *Sakel Fully Good Fair*. He pulls the broker's sample to pieces, picks out a greyish clump, takes hold of it with both hands, stretching it out between his thumbs until he finds out the length, colour and resistance of the fibre and how much waste matter it contains. He pushes it disdainfully aside and seizes another, examines it and then gives his verdict. He has been doing this every morning for a quarter of a century. His family can count a total of eighty-four years spent in Egypt, a fact of which he is proud. He is a native of one of the Greek islands. "It's extremely simple. A Lancashire spinner wants a thousand, or suppose even ten thousand bales of *Sakel* of our own mixture, which is our secret of course, delivery in November. *Va bene*. I immediately cover myself by a contract. I sell cotton that I don't possess six or seven times over. But at the end of November it has to be delivered. My price is guaranteed by contract. What about the difference you say? What if I can't find the cotton? In that case, my dear fellow, it's a very bad look out. It means that the market is strangled." Bells vibrate in the brokers' telephone boxes. I begin to understand their language.

Outside, the hurricane still rages. In the large *chounehs* belonging to the National Bank are rows of huge, fat bales with their seams bursting open, each one of which, labelled and tested, is the object of special care (when the temperature rises too high, a few small fuses bring down a timely shower from the ceiling); slit open by the classifier's knife, they await the time for *farfara* [hand-combing] and pressing. You can touch this long, fine, strong fibre which is made into useful textiles, tyres and no less useful explosives. It is not surprising that it is the object of a special cult. King Cotton is as rich as the Negus of Abyssinia, but his treasure is more cumbersome to carry away. Alexandria has good reason for worshipping it in Minet el-Bassal.

* * *

But in the centre of town, in Mohamed Ali Square, there is another temple devoted to a very different and less reasonable cult, the Stock Exchange. As you turn into Rue Cherif, your right ear drum is suddenly pierced by loud bawling. You think that someone is being murdered until you realize that the Alexandria businessmen are buying and selling shares, as they do all over the world, but here they usually deal in cotton contracts. This is the domain of the fictitious god of speculation, of a game, exciting "But relentless," interrupts my friend the broker. "It is not only an exciting game, it's a very hard struggle, without respite, in which you risk your life at any moment. The speculator may be a parasite but he is useful all the same. The Liverpool spinners need him, the exporters need him, and the fellahin need him. If there was no one to come in between the rise and the drop, to take the risk of future payment, to regularise the market by all sorts of wiles that you might call Machiavellian, to buy when there are no buyers and sell when there are no sellers, the *chounehs* would burst with the plenty, the cotton transports would give up and the Manchester looms grow rusty. Believe me, the speculator ought to be rehabilitated, although I, who am from Minet el-Bassal, do not like him. I even hate him. He is a bandit who assassinates his best friends in cold blood. When he goes bankrupt, in his turn, it is all part of the game."

After all, these two enclosures, one for contracts and the other for shares, these two broiling, yelling pits are the same in all the Stock Exchanges in the world. Though perhaps, here, the Oriental gesticulation adds a more Dantesque character to the scene. Perhaps also, the cry of the whole town can be heard. Egypt has the gambling fever, but here it is encountered in its purest form. Not only in the

Baudrot, celebrated tearoom and pastry shop at the corner of Rue Fouad and Rue Cherif Pacha.

Stock Exchange enclosure but in businessmen's offices, in lawyers' chambers and in cafés and places of amusement. It presides over work and pleasure. Pistachios won at the game of odds-and-evens taste better. A turkey is never more delicious than when won with a lottery ticket whilst seated round the table of a bar.

Young and old, men and women, everyone thinks of nothing but speculating. During the boom created by the war in 1914, Alexandria lived in a fever bordering on madness. You had only to sell the cotton mattress you slept on to enter the game. The prices on the Stock Exchange went up in vertical charts. A hundred thousand pounds profit in a few days made people lose their heads. And then everything crashed. But the fever still persists albeit in a very subdued form. Alexandria is still oversusceptible to invisible signals. On the slightest indication she goes from the deepest depression to the craziest of hopes. Alexandria has the nerves of a woman.

* * *

The true Alexandrian is, above all, a businessman. The kind of business matters little to him. His aim is to make money. Always on the lookout for a deal, he rapidly jots down figures on his cigarette box, makes an offer, withdraws, conceals his real intentions under a perpetual joviality, gets out of inextricable situations with surprising versatility, wavers between heights and depths and, as they say here, always "leaves a door open", if necessary puts up with makeshifts and cleverly gets out of bankruptcy.

He goes from his office to the Stock Exchange, thinking of nothing but his financial schemes, proffers his word of honour a hundred times a day, introduces into his fluent conversation words and expressions borrowed from the numerous languages he knows, but none of which he reveres, and forms neologisms without hesitation. He regards artistic emotions, philosophical research and the anguish experienced by people incapable of facing an arbitration as trash and nonsense. If you ask teachers who have brought up generations of Alexandrians, they will tell you with what rapidity the intellectual curiosity of even the most promising pupils gives way to orders issued by the Stock Exchange. Like the god Moloch, the Stock Exchange no longer counts its victims.

As all real gamblers, he is exceedingly superstitious. He believes in every kind of fetish and avoids starting certain negotiations on a Friday or meeting on the same day certain people reputed to have the evil eye.

In a poky office on the Rue de France, without any furniture except a safe and a telephone on the table, the owner makes rapid notes with his Eversharp, watches out for the invisible, nervously flicks the ash from his cigarette, and dreams: luck favours him. At the Café du Nil, four men talk as though delirious, gesticulating as if begging for mercy. Ill luck is dogging them. At Baudrot's, a dandy, assiduous in his attentions to some pretty women, quits them abruptly to start a conversation in the language of numbers at a neighbouring table: "How much is the February *Ashmuni*? And the November *Sakel Fully Good Fair*?" In a drawing room, in the middle of an exciting game of bridge, one of the players takes out his watch. It's midnight. Without troubling to apologize, he gets up and returns a moment later: he had to telephone to ask for the latest Liverpool quota. Women also speculate on the Stock Exchange and keep in daily contact with stock brokers. Others gravely play cards, morning, afternoon and night.

This passion for speculation which provides easy profit is accompanied by a desire for immediate material pleasures, such as the music hall and cinema.

The more sensible seek a necessary relaxation from the nervous strain by rowing in the port or camping in the desert. Although the

6813—The Sea Wall, Alexandria, Egypt.

The sea wall during the construction of the Corniche, 1905.

Alexandrian loves luxury, it is not so much for his own satisfaction as to show off. His office is often down a blind alley or in a backyard and contains only a plain wooden table and a cane chair. Sometimes, even though he possesses a car, he goes to work by tram, as long as no one sees him, standing on the platform because it is half price. Even if circumstances oblige him to reduce his mode of life, he is always to be met with on first nights in the cinemas and at the Sporting Club with his fashionably-dressed wife, careful above all to save social appearances which count in the business world. But should cotton go up twenty talaris: cars with chauffeurs, palatial residences, luxurious furniture, dresses, jewellery, receptions, holidays abroad, in short princely splendour. At such moments he spends freely and counts little, and everyone benefits.

For it should be said, in all justice, that the Alexandrian is clear-sighted, takes prompt decisions and bold initiatives and opens his hand with the gesture of a Maecenas. The Alexandrian is capable of making a donation of a hundred thousand pounds for the foundation of a hospital. Many more social welfare centres are created here than in Cairo and subsist thanks to his generosity.

He is more polished than the Cairene and prides himself on being more open-minded. He is proud of his city where people are more familiar with western civilization, a fact which, in his eyes, dubs him with a sort of aristocracy. He is also proud of the Alexandrian woman.

* * *

Alexandria has since her foundation ever been a cosmopolitan city. The Egyptians, apart from a few landowners and high Government officials, belong mostly to the working classes. The Italian colony from the Piazza della Paglia is composed chiefly of joiners, locksmiths, garage owners and foremen. Italians also flaunt the fascist badge in banks and shops where they are employed, sing the praise of Mussolini in schools or else make a living as doctors and lawyers. The best tailors and shoemakers are Armenians. The important firms of Matossian and Gamsaragan manufacture cigarettes. Syrians are not above sharing the small cotton trade with Jews. They both excel in the legal and medical professions and are generally successful in all sorts of jobs on the Stock Exchange and at Minet el-Bassal. They are shrewd speculators. The Jew, as a rule, dislikes manual work just as much in Alexandria as perhaps in Tel Aviv. At the most, he will agree to roll cigarettes and *macarona* for Coutarelli and Salonica. He prefers to figure amongst the unemployed and ask for charity, sell *lottaria* tickets and hawk cheap objects. To do you a favour, he may condescend to be a cashier in your bank or a salesman in your shop. As a small jeweller in the Sagha, an occupation already more to his taste, he is a passed master in dealing in silver and small loans. One step higher, he finds scope for his enterprising spirit in business, in the piece goods trade, *manufattura*, or even, as a last resort, in petty law suits. The Greeks, who since time immemorial, have constantly travelled to and fro between their islands and Egypt, feel quite at home here and have settled down everywhere in large numbers. The first European you see in a village is probably a Greek grocer, who is a money lender at the same time. They are amongst the first professional men in Alexandria and own the chief firms in the cotton export trade.

The British Empire is represented by its banks and The Eastern Telegraph. Amongst these Englishmen are many well-known businessmen: Alderson with his machines, Carver as an exporter and Barker as a shipowner. France has also several representatives among the veterans of the business world, along with bank managers, pedagogues, lawyers, engineers and the employers of Gaz Lebon. The Swiss occupy a front place among the exporters. The Belgians are centred round their bank.

When you think that in Cairo and in a number of provincial towns,

Imperial Airways seaplane *Scipio* in Alexandria Marine Airport, Ras el-Tin.

the same diversity of races, religions, and nationalities exists, you are inclined to say that Alexandria resembles them. There is however a difference. The foreign minorities or recently naturalized Egyptians there are lost among the Moslem masses by whom they are barely tolerated, here hold the levers of commercial activity and set the fashion in society.

Alone of its kind in Egypt, the administrative organization of the city has long offered a curiously international character. An organic status prohibiting more than three members of one nationality being elected on the Municipal Council is a significant feature, so that so-called "European" merchants, Greeks and Jews especially, claim the honour of having initiated measures taken to improve the aspect and hygiene of the town and of raising it to its present level.

How do these various ethnic elements carry themselves? A superficial observer might have a wrong impression from the fact that they appear so scattered. Without mentioning isolated groups like the English who meet no one but each other at the Sporting Club, and even the French who have no time for social life and think of nothing but economising for their return to France, the foreigners, even the most adapted to Egyptian life, even the most Orientalised of them, still cling steadfastly to their own characteristics. They all belong to carefully organised communities, each of which has its own churches or synagogues, its own clergy, schools, hospitals and cemeteries, and whose weddings and christening ceremonies and "personal status" are each definitely distinct.

Notions of race and religion are mixed, or rather are stronger here than elsewhere. For example, a Jew, whether Sephardi or Ashkenazi, whether from Morocco, Smyrna, Salonika, Syria or Italy, is always a Jew, and lives amongst his own community: his nationality, which often is a mere question of passport, means little. Two Syrians, whether of the same origin or not, when one is descended from the Crusaders and the other from the khalifs, are entirely different, since one professes the Catholic religion and the other that of Islam, the latter losing his identity amongst the Egyptian Moslems. This seems most astonishing to a European, for whom the word nationality has a meaning at the same time strict and mystical.

It might be thought that daily intercourse would efface or at least lessen differences of race and religion. But the contrary is the case. The Jews insist on closing their offices for Purim, the French celebrate the 14th of July, the English Empire Day, the Greeks St. George's Day, and the Italians the anniversary of the March on Rome. A Frenchman, even if he does not practice his religion in France, here attends Consular Mass and is buried in his own cemetery. On the day of Kippur, the Jewish crowd ostensibly invades the Rue Nabi Daniel, each man carrying under his arm a velvet bag containing the *talet* and the Holy Book. On Palm Sunday, the Copts go about the streets waving plaited palm leaves. On Good Friday, the traffic in Rue Fouad is held up by a Greek Orthodox procession whose bareheaded members wave banners and incense burners in the air. They are accompanied by long-haired Greek papas, their Bishop and their Consul. And nothing is more common than to see a Moslem stop at the corner of a public square, take off his shoes, raise his arms and bend down in prayer on the pavement without paying the slightest attention to the passersby. The expression "of no religion" is incomprehensible and denotes a monstrosity.

* * *

At teatime, the Alexandria Sailing Club is full of smart women seated on one of three terraces as though it were a theatre. The western seafront which opens before them provides a diversion or at least an agreeable subject for their dreams. The background is too far away to be of interest: Agamy, the Mex desert, the tanneries whose horrible smell fortunately does not come this far, the tanks of Vacuum Oil, the funny aerial trucks of the very smoky coal quay, the dense crowd on the marine quay and beyond, their beloved and blamed town with its domino-like houses set up in rows along the water's edge. This is all very far away, but it is a pleasure to look at the spruce *Mahroussa* with its green-edged white hull, its yellow funnel and shining brass work, awaiting Royal pleasure. Even the old-fashioned, black and white training ship, the *Faroukia*, its masts and sails erect against a lovely pale sky, is worth a glance. On the right are the smart Sailing Club and the Rowing Club, which is really not at all bad. The small craft dotted about on the waves with their double lateen sails forming white patches round old, half-sunk barges, add a pleasant touch of gaiety to the scene. There is no lack of choice of bark if a sail is desired. Cutters, yawls and dinghies. Sailors repainting their hulls are heard whistling. Life seems sweet. Here is the *Marco Polo* moving off with all its passengers on deck. It is bound for Naples. What a temptation! You feel inclined to go as far as the pontoon, to jump into a boat and dive into the deep water, far away, though not too far, from the troublesome crowd. The large white seaplane belonging to the Imperial Airways, coming from Mirabelle, steers round and falls on its floats, splashing water around it. You think of your mail that is due, but you do not attempt to move. The surf behind you continues its monotonous murmur, with a suggestion of melancholy just sufficient for perfect happiness. The setting sun in its turn splashes the top of the lighthouse. It is time for another cigarette. The harbour is certainly a relief from the vulgarity of the beaches.

Imperial Airways advertisements 1939.

The Cosmopolitan Identity

Robert Mabro

Alexandria was a fragmented society, and not only along the Egyptian/foreigner boundary. The foreigners did not form a homogenous group. Those who had a clear national identity held to it: this was the hard core of their inner being. Those who generated the Alexandrian cosmopolitan identity mixed together in cultural events and could talk to each other about certain intellectual issues. But the *shawam* remained *shawam,* the Italians remained Italians, and the Jews remained Jews. Exogamy existed but was frowned upon. Conversions from one religion to another occurred but were rare.

The area of social intercourse was business. The areas that were taboo were religion and politics.

The ambiguity of social life in cosmopolitan Alexandria lay in the co-existence of openness in economic life and closed boundaries elsewhere. Relationships could only develop in neutral areas between the many walls. Hence the need to tread cautiously and the impression that social life was a lazy, pleasant but very careful dance. The impression was created—and people came to believe—that 'we are all happy together'. The pace of the dance was never accelerated, lest the feeling of superficial happiness should collapse through some *faux pas.* And the golden rule was never to talk seriously, if at all, about the things that mattered most: differences in values, or in religious or political perspective.

And the ambiguity of identity for those who belonged to the cosmopolitan culture lay in the co-existence of a hard core of strongly held beliefs and dearly cherished personal interests at the centre and an ill-defined fringe all around. It was the fringe that related the members of the cosmopolitan group to another. But within that fringe there was little of real substance – some illusions and dreams, some common negative elements of self-definition. The fringe had no boundaries. It was rather like the long coastline of Alexandria which opens it to the Mediterranean but is not a frontier with any particular country.

And it was the coast which reminded Alexandrians, when they turned their sights on the sea, that otherness was the source of their inner trouble. Otherness was just beyond a distant but neatly drawn blue horizon. But otherness could not be reached by dreaming of this beyond while lazing on the beaches. The sea which put them in touch with otherness, through intimation, brought them back, as on the returning wave, to Alexandria, and to the hard core of the self. The ambiguity of the Alexandrian identity resides perhaps in this feeling that otherness was its true nature but that true otherness was not attainable. Egyptians constantly reminded the foreigner that he or she was 'another'. The Alexandrian foreigner, immersed for several generations in the city, might also have liked to be 'another', but in many cases had no choice, and none of these foreigners could really *be* the 'other' that they thought they were.

Alexandrian belle at the beach.

Sources

Amicale Alexandrie Hier et Aujourd'hui. http://www.aaha.ch

Awad, Mohamed. *Italy in Alexandria: Influences on the built environment.* Alexandria Preservation Trust, 2008. (Reprinted by permission of the author.)

Breccia, Evaristo. *Alexandria Ad Aegyptum: A Guide to the Ancient and Modern Town and to its Graeco-Roman Museum.* Instituto Italiano d'Arti Grafiche, Bergamo,.1922. (Courtesy McGill University Library.)

Breccia, Sandro. *Le Port d'Alexandrie.* Société Royale d'Archéologie d'Alexandrie, 1926. (Courtesy Bibliothèque Nationale de France.) Translated by Susan Glynn.

Butler, Alfred Joshua. *Court Life in Egypt.* London: Chapman and Hall, 1887.

Cavafy, C. P. *Collected Poems*, translated by Edmund Keeley and Philip Sherrard. Princeton University Press, 1992. (Reprinted by permission of Taylor & Francis Ltd.)

Forster, E. M. *Alexandria: A History and a Guide.* Whitehead Morris, 1922. (Reprinted by permission of The Provost and Scholars of King's College, Cambridge and the Society of Authors as the E.M. Forster Estate.)

François-Levernay, E. *Guide Annuaire d'Egypte: statistique, administrations, commerce, industries, agriculture, antiquités etc., avec les plans d'Alexandrie et du Caire : année 1872–1873.* Cairo. (Courtesy Bibliothèque Nationale de France.) Translated by Maya Massaad.

Glavanis, Pandelis. "Aspects of the Economic and Social History of the Greek Community in Alexandria during the 19th Century." Ph.D. thesis, University of Hull, 1989.

Guerville, A. B. de. *New Egypt.* London: William Heinemann, 1906.

La Réforme. *50 Ans de Vie d'Egypte à travers La Réforme, Le Livre d'Or du Journal La Réforme 1895–1945.* Alexandrie, 1945. Translated by Maya Massaad.

Lackany, Radames S. *Notes sur quelques nomenclatures Alexandrines.* Cahiers d'Alexandrie, 1964.

Lackany, Radames. *Quatre Espagnols à Alexandrie au Moyen Age.* Conference donnée au Centre Hispanique d'Alexandrie, 1968.

Leprette, Fernand. *Egypt Land of the Nile,* translated from the French by Lillian Goar, Cairo: R. Schindler, 1940.

Lively, Penelope. *Oleander, Jacaranda: A Childhood Perceived: A Memoir.* HarperCollins, 1994.

Mabro, Robert. "Alexandria 1860–1960: The Cosmopolitan Identity." In *Alexandria, Real and Imagined*, edited by Anthony Hirst and Michael Silk. Routledge, 2004 (reproduced by arrangement with Taylor & Francis Books UK).

Mansel, Philip. "The Rise and Fall of Royal Alexandria: From Mohammed Ali to Farouk." In *The Court Historian*, Vol. 17, Issue 2, 2012. (Reprinted by permission of Taylor & Francis Ltd on behalf of The Society for Court Studies.)

Manzoni, Sandro. "Les Juifs d'Alexandrie." In *Amicale Alexandrie Hier et Aujourd'hui*, Cahier nº 65, November 2011.

Murphy, Mike. "Notes on Some Alexandrian Names." In *The Egypt Study Circle*, Volume XXI Nº 3, September 2011.

Pecnik, Charles. *Ramleh, La Riviera Eleusinienne et Alexandrie (Egypte).* Léon Woerl, 1901. (Courtesy Bibliothèque Nationale de France.) Translated by Maya Massaad.

Raafat, Samir. egy.com. (Reprinted by permission of the author.)

Solé, Robert. *Birds of Passage.* Harvill, 2000.

The Mahmoudieh Canal. The New York Times, August 20, 1882.

Toussoun, Omar. *Tārīkh khalīj al-Iskandarīyah al-qadīm wa tur'at al-Maḥmūdīyah* by 'Umar Ṭūsūn, 1942 — being an Arabic translation of *Memoire sur l'histoire du Nil* by Prince Omar Toussoun, Mémoires présentés à l'Institut égyptien, 1925. Translated by Nada Baroud.

Van Pellecom, Ronny, Peter Grech, and Alain Stragier. *Alexandria Ramleh: Its Development and Postal History, 1863–1929,* 2015.

Zimmerli Hardman, Esther. *From Camp Caesar to Cleopatra's Pool: A Swiss Childhood in Alexandria, 1934–1950.* Bibliotheca Alexandrina, 2008.

Images

Alinari: 56, 57, 58, 59, 199, 200, 201, 205; Alf van Beem, Wikimedia Commons: 141; The American University in Cairo Rare Books and Special Collections Library: 29, 30, 31, 32, 33; Bibliothèque Nationale de France: front endpaper, 9, 11, 13, 15, 17, 19, 21, 23, 25, 54, 69, 163, 221, cover (Alexander); Centre d'Études Alexandrines (CEAlex): back endpaper, 27, 165; ELIA/MIET Photographic Archive: 64, 67, 77, 91, 98, 99, 113, 117, 119, 124, 129, 133, 143, 169, 189, 196, 208, 209, 226; Library of Congress: 6, 35, 97, 121, 123, 132, 134, 135, 211, 229, 243, 247, 249; Michael Bates: cover (Mohamed Ali); Paul Geday: 73, 195; Pierre Sioufi Collection: 39, 46, 47, 49, 51, 52, 53, 70, 71, 81, 83, 84, 85, 86, 87, 88, 89, 90, 92, 93, 101, 103, 104, 105, 109, 115, 116, 127, 128, 131, 147, 148, 150, 151, 153, 155, 156, 157, 167, 171, 175, 179, 181, 183, 185, 187, 191, 197, 207, 213, 222, 227; Private Collection: 4, 37, 41, 43, 45, 55, 61, 63, 65, 75, 79, 92, 95, 106, 107, 110, 111, 125, 126, 137, 139, 145, 149, 159, 161, 173, 177, 188, 190, 193, 214, 215, 217, 219, 223, 224, 225, 233, 235, 237, 239, 241, 245, 251, 253, 256.

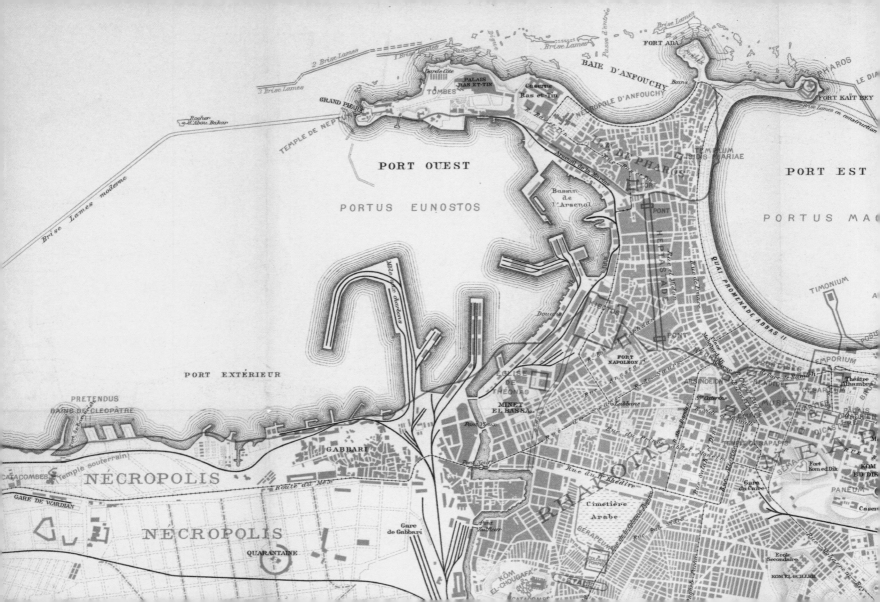